When Love Returns

Kay D. Rizzo

Pacific Press Publishing Association
Boise, Idaho
Oshawa, Ontario, Canada

Edited by Randy Maxwell
Designed by Tim Larson
Cover by Lars Justinen
Type set in 10/11 Century Schoolbook

Copyright © 1987 by
Pacific Press Publishing Association
Printed in United States of America
All Rights Reserved

Library of Congress Catalog Card Number: 87-62590

ISBN 0-8163-0771-7

88 89 90 91 • 5 4 3 2

Dedication

To
Richard,
my forever friend.

Contents

1. Change of Plans — 5
2. The Right Choice — 10
3. Tall Tales and Good-Night Kisses — 17
4. Bears in the Night — 24
5. A Thorn in the Flesh — 29
6. The Picnic — 35
7. Call in the Night — 43
8. Facing the Facts — 50
9. Grizzly! — 55
10. Silver Skates — 62
11. Christmas Holidays — 66
12. Fighting the Blizzard — 70
13. Mrs. Karpenko—For a Moment — 73
14. Life in the Arctic — 78
15. Letting Go — 85
16. Time to Retreat — 89
17. When Love Returns — 92

Chapter 1
Change of Plans

Kelli Saunders picked up the receiver, her gaze moving from the half-finished letter in the typewriter to the blossoming lilac bush beyond the window.

"English Department. Dr. Sawyer's office. May I help you?"

"So efficient!" A chuckle came over the line causing a tender smile to curve Kelli's lips.

"Jeff! I didn't expect to hear from you for at least another hour." She glanced at the clock above her desk. A quarter past four—forty-five minutes and three letters to finish before she could sign out of work.

"I just couldn't wait until supper to talk with you, Sweetheart. I've got some good news for you," he added excitedly.

"I could stand a little good news, I think," Kelli sighed, recalling the disappointment she'd felt when the prospects for her first teaching job after graduation crumbled. Emerson Academy, an elite school for girls in Connecticut, was, at first, eager to hire Kelli as an English, art, and interior design teacher for their seventh and eighth graders. The offer excited Kelli because it meant living within moderate driving distance of Maryland, where her fiancé, Jeff Morgan, would be a first-year medical student.

"Can I come over to the office, or can you meet me at the cafeteria right away?" Jeff asked excitedly.

"I'm sorry, but I have to get these letters done before I leave. Dr. Sawyer wants to get them out in tomorrow's mail. Can you tell me over the phone?" Kelli positioned the receiver between her shoulder and neck and began typing the rest of the letter she'd started earlier.

"Aw, I guess," Jeff muttered, a martyred whine entering his voice. "I talked with my parents, and they've agreed to support us if we get married this summer and go back to Maryland together. You could pick up some sort of job to keep you busy until a teaching position opens up. Isn't that great?"

"It's very nice of your folks to agree to such a plan, but, well, I don't know—" She hesitated, feeling extremely uncomfortable with the prospect of depending on Jeff's wealthy and often interfering parents for her livelihood.

"Aw come on, Kelli," Jeff whined. "You're just stalling on marrying me. You don't really love me enough, do you?"

"Jeff," Kelli interrupted, a wrinkle of irritation creasing her brow, "if I didn't love you, I wouldn't have accepted your proposal of marriage. It's just—oh I don't know. Let me think it over and pray about it for a while, OK?"

The silence that followed made Kelli wonder if Jeff had hung up. Finally he spoke, "Well, I guess so." She could tell from the tone of his voice that Jeff was pouting. Being the only son of a wealthy entrepreneur, Jeff grew up with more than his share of advantages and few deprivations. This worried Kelli since her parents had trained their two daughters to work hard for the things they wanted.

"Will I see you at suppertime?" she asked.

"I don't know," he growled. "I don't have to tell you how disappointed I am at your reaction."

Kelli sighed and bit her lip. "Whatever. I'll have to run these letters over to the placement office for Dr. Sawyer before five, so I'd better hang up now."

"Fine. Bye." The line went dead. She shook her head and hung up the receiver. Another glance at the clock told her that she had less than thirty-five minutes to finish the remaining letters and run them to the other office before it closed. Kelli wore a troubled frown as she finished the letter. For some undefinable reason, she felt uneasy. Maybe it wasn't such a big deal to have Jeff's parents support them while he attended medical school. Most of the premed students were planning similar strategies or else planning to take out giant government loans to finance their education.

"I must learn to trust Jeff's judgment more," she thought, "if I'm going to spend the rest of my life with him." Sometimes Kelli found Jeff to be such a little boy. But that was also part of his charm—except when he wanted to get his way. Then she didn't find him quite so charming.

Easygoing and jocular, Jeff possessed the good looks and sense of humor that women found attractive, Kelli included. Before the first week of their senior year had passed, they were a steady item on campus. Within six weeks of their first date, Jeff had proposed. Kelli had managed to stall him until Valentine's Day, when he declared his intentions before the entire student body. Embarrassed, yet flattered, Kelli agreed to his proposal.

When he was accepted at Johns Hopkins University and she'd landed the teaching position in Connecticut, they planned to marry during the Christmas break. But since losing the teaching assignment, their plans had been tabled—until now.

Kelli's uneasiness persisted as she finished the letters and hurried across campus to the administration building, determined to beat the five o'clock deadline. She stepped into the office just as the secretary was covering her typewriter for the night.

"Hi, Sue," Kelli said, dropping the stack of letters on the desk. "Here are the letters Dr. Sawyer wants Miss Andrews to approve and mail tomorrow morning."

"Great. Miss Andrews has been waiting for them. Let me buzz her. Then I'll walk you to the cafeteria, or is Jeff meeting you?"

"No, he isn't. I'd like to walk with you," Kelli admitted. She moved to the narrow window overlooking the main section of campus. Behind her, she heard a voice on the intercom.

"Sue, has Kelli Saunders arrived yet with Dr. Sawyer's letters?"

Kelli turned around just as Sue answered.

"Yes, she's here right now."

"Good! Please send her in to see me."

Sue nodded toward the door at the other side of the room.

As she turned the doorknob, Kelli whispered to her friend, "Wait for me, OK? I'll be right out."

Sue agreed.

Miss Andrews looked up from the stack of papers on her desk as Kelli entered. "Oh, I'm so glad I caught you. Take a seat for a moment. I'll be right with you."

Kelli smiled and sat down.

Miss Andrews pulled a letter from the middle of the stack and nodded. "Yes, this is the one," she muttered. "I received a letter today that might interest you. Have you made plans for next school year since the Emerson Academy position fell through?"

"No, Ma'am, not yet. I guess I keep hoping something will turn up before graduation."

"Well, maybe it has," Miss Andrews began. "This letter is from a Mrs. Karpenko in behalf of her three grandchildren. They need a tutor—in Alaska, for a year. I realize that it's not the same as a bona fide teaching position, but it might tide you over for one year until Emerson becomes available. Are you interested?"

Kelli blinked back her surprise. "Well, I'd need to know a bit more about the situation before I made a decision."

"Of course," the middle-aged woman agreed. "Here's Mrs. Karpenko's letter." She handed the letter to Kelli. "I called the three individuals she listed for references before I even considered presenting it to you. And they speak highly of the woman and her son, Dr. Karpenko. You will, of course, want to talk with them also before you make an irrevocable decision."

Kelli scanned the letter as the woman continued speaking.

"As you can see, it would be just an interim measure—a one-year proposition. But the pay is good, and unless you and Jeff are getting married sooner than a year from now, it could be a great adventure for a young woman like you—living in Alaska."

Kelli shook her head, wondering what her parents would think. It did sound enticing to spend a year in Alaska—kind of an off-beat sort of interlude between college and entering the legitimate working world. "Yeah, that's it—an Alaskan interlude." She smiled to herself, then frowned. What would Jeff say?

Suddenly she realized that Miss Andrews was waiting for her to reply.

"Could I have a copy of this letter?" Kelli asked. "I'd like to think this over, check out the references as you suggested, and talk with my parents and fiancé about it before I say anything definite."

"That's fair enough," Miss Andrews agreed. "I'll have Sue make a copy for you. I will need to know as soon as possible in order to fill the position should you decline."

"Could I have until Monday morning to think about it?"

"That sounds reasonable. Shall we say ten o'clock?"

By the time Sue and Kelli emerged from the college administration building, Sue was bursting with curiosity. "Well?"

"A job for me—in Alaska of all places!" Kelli squealed. "I'd be sort of a governess/tutor for three children, twin girls age ten and a five-year-old boy," Kelli explained.

Sue stopped and stared. "What! You turned her down, didn't you? She should know you wouldn't even consider such a position with Jeff studying in Maryland next year."

"I—I don't know. I told her I'd think about it over the weekend. I have to let her know by Monday," Kelli admitted as she fell into step with her friend.

"You're joking! You'd risk losing a hunk like Jeff for the privilege of being stranded in Alaska for nine months?" Sue asked, her face darkening with incredulity.

"I don't know. I just don't know right now." Kelli shoved her hands deep into her jacket pockets and stared straight ahead at the empty sidewalk.

Sue chuckled and nodded her head slowly. "Well, you'd better decide soon 'cause Jeff is waiting by the cafeteria entrance."

Throughout supper, Jeff rehashed his and his parents' latest plans concerning the wedding and living expenses, hardly aware of Kelli's preoccupation. When he finally ran out of words and she still hadn't said anything, he looked at her. "Hey, what is it?" Jeff asked. "You haven't heard a word I've said during the entire meal, and you've barely touched your food. What's wrong? Are you sick or something?"

Kelli took a sip of water to moisten her mouth, which felt like it had been stuffed with cotton batting. Hesitant, she explained about her visit with Miss Andrews and the unusual offer she'd received. "I haven't had time to even pray about this yet, and, of course, I'd like to talk with my folks before I made a decision."

Jeff stiffened, his jaw jutting forward. "Decision? Is there any doubt? I'll make it for you—no! I won't agree to your going to Alaska for a year while I'm in Maryland. No. Forget it. How could Miss Andrews have even suggested such a thing?"

"Hey, wait a minute," Kelli said, barely speaking above a whisper. "This is my decision to make, Jeff. Of course, I want your input, but ultimately, I must decide."

"You're willing to throw away our happiness to take this job?" Jeff's eyes flashed with anger as he snatched their trays and left Kelli sitting at the table.

Kelli hurried after him, trying to explain. "I didn't say I was taking the job. I just said, I needed to think and pray about it before I decide."

"That you would even consider such a thing proves to me that you don't love me anywhere near as much as I do you," he called over his shoulder, as he headed down the sidewalk toward the men's dormitory.

A misty rain started to fall as Kelli angled across the lawn toward the women's dormitory. "Maybe you're right, Jeff. Maybe you're right," she muttered as she wiped an unwelcome tear from her cheek.

Chapter 2
The Right Choice

The wings dipped low over the icy blue lake as the single-engine Cessna Stationair circled to land in the clearing that temporarily divided the unending forests of Northern Hemlock. Kelli strained to catch a glimpse of her new home. Excitement danced in her eyes. Though she was certain that she must resemble a young child at Christmas with her nose pasted to the toy-store window, she couldn't contain her enthusiasm. Almost as an afterthought, she tightened the seat belt across her shoulder and lap.

"Secure? It will take more than a seat belt to bring any security back into my life," she admitted. "Any security I might have had, I left in Seattle this morning." Yet, even as butterflies played tag within her stomach, her mother's voice echoed through her mind.

"In all thy ways acknowledge him, and he shall direct thy paths." Proverbs 3:6. Kelli had no doubt that her parents' lives revolved around that promise.

When Kelli chose to attend a small Christian college more than 400 miles from home instead of the state university less than a mile from her house, when she decided to become an elementary teacher instead of a news journalist, when she postponed marriage to Jeff in order to take this tutoring job on the Alaskan frontier, the promise served as her guide also.

Questions tumbled through her mind faster than she could organize them. What would the children be like? Would they obey her—like her? Were they bright—quick to learn? And what about their father, Dr. Peter Karpenko? Young? Middle-aged? Bookish? Grouchy? Aloof? Was he the stereotypical scientist, lost in his own world?

The rakishly handsome pilot raised one eyebrow, as Kelli nervously twisted and untwisted the excess seatbelt strap. She failed to notice that his glance skimmed over her neatly tailored, berry-red pants and matching jacket. Kelli's foot tapped out a message of impatience; her face registering apprehension. Through her long, dark lashes, she caught him in the middle of his rather thorough appraisal.

He grinned. "They won't bite, you know—at least not Grandma and the children. Now Peter, he's something else. He's been known to growl, roar, and rampage, all in one breath. And he's sworn off marriage. So beware!"

The pilot's cockeyed grin broadened at the sight of her irritated blush. "Take me, for instance. I'm a sucker for a pretty face. And I'm ripe for the picking. I might like settling down if it meant staring across the breakfast table at a purty thing like you."

"Mr. Lee," Kelli patiently explained, "I am not in Alaska to find a husband. If that were my goal, I could have accomplished it while in college. I am engaged to a first-year medical student in Maryland."

"Infuriating man! Why am I telling this complete stranger about Jeff," she wondered as the pilot's attention returned to landing the plane. "And who cares if Dr. Peter Karpenko wants to remain single or not? Surely not me!"

The pilot eased up on the throttle and chuckled. "For a medical student, he's not very bright—allowing his woman to come up here to wolf country, alone and single. Doubt he'll ever get you to the altar."

Kelli's lips tightened. Her deep brown eyes flashed indignantly. "Mr. Lee—" she began.

"Call me Roger."

"Mr. Lee, perhaps your line has worked in the past, but I think you should know I'm not the type of girl to change my affections with my hairstyle. Jeff trusts me implicitly, as I trust him. Thank you, however, for the compliment."

"Oh, you're welcome, I'm sure. A year is a long time; a lot can happen in twelve months. Remember, you heard that from me."

By now Kelli's foot danced to an inner war chant. She pursed her lips and glared silently at the control panel.

"Oh, now wait. Let me finish before you get huffy. I'm trying to be nice. I was going to add that if you don't like staying with the Karpenkos, I'm only twenty miles away, at the trading post. Of course, those twenty miles are over hazardous terrain, but what's a little terra firma between friends?"

A stray lock of shoulder-length, brown hair graced Kelli's cheek, its red highlights glistening in the sunlight. She pushed it aside and tilted her chin defiantly. "I'm confident that I will not need your most generous offer, thank you."

His mocking grin slid easily back into place. "Ready or not, here come your charges. They've been pestering me about you all week."

Just as the plane touched down, she turned in time to see two girls race across the landing strip. "So those are the twins," Kelli thought, as the Cessna rolled to a stop. "They sure do look alike."

A smaller boy struggled to keep up with the girls, managing to trip and fall over a dirt clod in his pathway. Kelli grinned as she watched the child pick himself up, dust off the knees of his jeans, and begin running again.

"Well, here goes." Kelli took a deep breath, allowing the pilot to help her from the cockpit.

"Don't worry, Sweetheart. They're great kids. Give them lots of love, and they'll love ya back," he whispered, as if reading the fear in her heart.

"Hey, Pamela," Roger called to the tallest of the three children, "how's Grandma feeling today?"

"Her head ached this morning, but she's doing better now." The blond, pony-tailed girl eyed Kelli, as if sizing up a competitor.

Her sister, a slightly smaller version, edged her way into the group and sidled up to the pilot.

"Well, hi there, Peanut." Roger tugged on the second girl's ponytail. "This here's your new school teacher, Kelli Saunders. Lisa, meet Kelli. Kelli, meet Lisa." A shy, tentative hand reached out to Kelli's.

"Hi, Lisa, I've been so anxious to meet you. Mr. Lee had a hard time keeping me in the plane. He was flying so slowly, I wanted to hop out and run on ahead."

"Oops," Kelli thought, "I'm trying too hard. Back off a bit."

"And you must be Pamela." The girl ignored Kelli's outstretched hand. Instead, Pamela lifted the boy into her arms.

The boy greeted her with, "Hello, Miss Saunders. I'm Petey. Have you really come to take my mommy's place?"

Kelli's mouth dropped open in horror; then she hastened to assure him, "No Petey. I'm not here to take your mother's place. No one can ever do that. I'm just here to help you learn to read and write and to—"

"Like I've been teaching you," Pamela interrupted. "Daddy and Grandma think an adult can do a better job."

Impatient with his older sister, Petey slipped out of her grasp and raced back across the clearing. "She's here, Grandma!" He yelled as he ran.

Lisa reached for Kelli's luggage. "Let me help you." Pamela

glared at Lisa, then stomped off toward the break in the trees.

Kelli looked questioningly at Roger. "What . . . ?"

He shrugged his shoulders, then bellowed, "Pamela! Get yourself back here and help me carry these packages to the cabin. No one goes off empty-handed." Then to Lisa, he added, "Tell your dad that I'll put his new tools in the storage shed." He pointed toward a small wooden building off to one side of the airstrip.

Still miffed by Pamela's behavior, Kelli started at Lisa's voice. "I'll take you to the cabin. And don't mind Pamela. Daddy says her nose is out of joint. She's been the big boss around here whenever Grandma had to go to Anchorage, and now she won't be, that's all."

Kelli had pictured a rough-hewn log cabin built on stilts to accommodate the Alaskan winter snows. She'd imagined it to have two or three rooms at the most, and perhaps a loft. So when Kelli spotted the "cabin," she stopped, stunned by the sight before her.

Lisa noticed Kelli's look of surprise. "What's wrong?"

"That's the cabin?" Kelli asked incredulously.

"Yep. Daddy built it the summer after Mama died. Later, he and Grandma brought us up here from California."

A large, native-wood A-frame towered high above her head. The floor-to-ceiling windows commanded a panoramic view of the airstrip, lake, and mountain range beyond.

"The addition off to the left is Daddy's laboratory," Lisa added importantly. "He's a geologist, you know. He built an addition on the back for Grandma. She has her own sitting room and bathroom and everything."

"You're pretty proud of your daddy, aren't you?" Kelli encouraged. "And obviously you should be. It's a beautiful home."

A woman of medium height with graying hair, dressed in a blue housedress and yellow calico apron came out onto the expansive deck that wrapped around the front of the house.

"Hi, Miss Saunders. I'm Grandma Karpenko." In spite of the woman's sunny welcome, Kelli could see traces of pain reflected in her eyes.

"I'm so glad to finally meet you," Kelli admitted. "After all our correspondence, I feel like I already know you."

"Come right on in."

"Thank you." Kelli followed the older woman into the cabin.

"Roger, Peter will be wanting those boxes in the lab," Mrs. Karpenko suggested. "He's been waiting for this equipment for over three months. Just stack them inside the door. Then, would you please take Miss Saunders' luggage upstairs to the guest room?"

Kelli paused to survey the carefully appointed living room. "What a perfect interlude," she thought. "What fantastic memories I'll take home with me next spring." A large double-seated rocking chair sat to one side of a gigantic stone fireplace. Opposite the chair was an overstuffed sofa one could get lost in. An ebony baby grand piano held center stage in front of the floor-to-ceiling window. Various seating arrangements distributed about the room completed the homey environment.

"Now, I'm sure you're tired from your long journey. So why don't you unpack, take a bath, and rest a while if you'd like. We'll see you at suppertime. Peter should be here by six tonight. Regardless, we'll sit down to eat at six-thirty. Now scoot, and don't you children bother Miss Saunders until then, do you hear?

"But Grandma—" Petey whined.

"Grandma's right," Pamela snapped. Kelli wondered why she sensed that Pamela didn't have her best welfare in mind.

"Miss Saunders hasn't met Benjamin yet," Petey insisted.

"There'll be plenty of time for her to meet Benjamin," Grandma replied. "The children's rooms are just beyond yours. You'll share a bathroom with them. I hope that's all right."

"Of course. What's sharing a bathroom with three children compared with sharing one with more than three hundred girls in a dormitory?"

Kelli skipped up the flight of stairs, anxious to see the room assigned to her. "Ooh, how lovely!" she gasped upon entering the large, airy bed-sitting room.

"Thank you," Roger quipped, placing her baggage by the closet door. "I've always considered myself rather lovely. I'm glad you agree."

Kelli shook her head and laughed. "You are incorrigible, Sir, quite incorrigible." She dropped her travel bag and purse onto the kingsize four-poster bed. Unable to resist, she bounced once or twice on the edge of the bed.

"This room must be at least a quarter the size of the entire second floor," she mused. The kaleidoscope of colors in the homemade crazy quilt brightened the varnished wall paneling. Fluffy, white priscilla curtains spoke of home and loving care. A granny rocker faced the window. "Yes," she thought, "a perfect interlude before picking up the pattern of my life again!"

Roger snapped his fingers in front of her eyes. "Hey, are you ignoring me? Kelli?"

"Huh? What? Oh, I'm sorry. Were you saying something? I wasn't listening," Kelli admitted sheepishly.

"Obviously! I asked if you would go on a picnic with me to Blue Hill Pass next weekend? The scenery's great. So's the company!"

"Perhaps I'd better take a rain check until I know the routine around here and understand what's expected of me," Kelli demurred, hoping not to give offense.

"Don't worry, I can handle rejection," Roger drawled, leaning against the doorjamb. "Well, I've got to be getting back to the store. See you in a few days when I deliver groceries."

Finally Kelli was alone. She opened her first suitcase. On top of her clothes was a small, porcelain-framed motto her mother had bought her for her dorm room the first year Kelli left for college.

It said, "If you love something, set it free. If it never returns, it was not yours in the first place. If it returns, it is yours forever."

Kelli had read that saying repeatedly during the weeks preceding her flight north. She thought of Jeff and the risk of letting him go east without her.

Kelli kicked off her shoes and leaned back onto the soft, downy quilt. She glanced toward the alarm clock she'd brought with her and thought of her mother and father sitting in the living room for family worship.

Her father's deep, resonant bass voice surfaced in her mind. "Alaska? Of all places," her father had groaned.

"I'd feel much better about the position at that Connecticut girls' school," her mother added.

Then her father's voice broke into her thoughts again, "I don't see why you can't apply to substitute teach here in the valley, or perhaps begin a master's program at the university."

"Dad, I'm not ready to begin a master's program. I need some experience first. And as for substitute teaching, do you really think I'd be happy sitting around waiting for the phone to ring?" Kelli argued. "When Jeff leaves for medical school, I'll have even more time on my hands. There are no teaching opportunities in southern Oregon right now. I'm twenty-two years old. Most of the girls from my high-school graduating class are married and have babies already," she reminded. "The job is only temporary—one year. After that, who knows? I'll probably marry Jeff and teach somewhere in the East."

"Dear," Mother interrupted, "please understand. It's painful to see our last little chick fly the coop. But you're right. I was married and already pregnant with Rhonda at twenty-two."

"Humph!" Dad grunted. "That was different!" When both women giggled, he laughed in spite of himself.

"Dad, no matter how old I get, I'll always be your baby, right? I've prayed about this all weekend, and it's something I feel I must do. I honestly believe the Lord is leading me to Alaska. Aren't you the one who taught me the verse, 'In all thy ways acknowledge him'?" Kelli gently reminded.

A close family, the Saunders sustained a strong bond of communication with their two daughters that lasted from infancy through the often turbulent teenage years. Even now, both young women valued their parents' advice.

"What do you know about this Karpenko anyway? Who knows what will happen once he gets you up there alone?"

"I checked out their references and have received nothing but excellent reports. Dr. Karpenko is on leave from Cal Tech, doing government research. I've prayed about it, and at every turn, I seem to be led right back to this job. Dr. Karpenko's mother lives at the cabin along with the three children," Kelli emphasized, trying to ease her parents' anxiety over her proposed adventure, especially her father's. "Dad, you know how much I love teaching, and I'm a good teacher. But with the job shortage, it's hard to get a chance to prove it."

"Someday, you'll understand how difficult it is for parents to let go," her father sighed. "No matter how well you think you've planned for the day, you're never really ready. But you're right. Follow God's guidance. Our blessings and prayers are with you."

"Thanks, Dad. I need both desperately."

Kelli's reverie shifted once again to Jeff. He had called, determined to try one more time to argue her out of going to Alaska, but she remained firm.

"I'm sorry, Jeff. Maybe I need time on my own for a while before I jump into marriage," she suggested. An abrupt goodbye ended the conversation. After graduation, though technically engaged, a definite chill had set in their relationship.

Slowly, Kelli's thoughts returned to her present location in the land of northern lights and dog-sled races. She crossed the room and swept the ruffled curtain aside to face the encroaching forest.

"Thank You, Lord, for leading me here," she whispered. "Help me to fulfill Your plans for me."

A short, rumpled figure with eyes upturned stood beneath her window. As soon as Petey spied a movement at the curtains, he waved. "Sleep well, Miss Kelli. I've got to go now because Grandma said I shouldn't bother you. Bye."

Smiling, Kelli hauled the first of her three suitcases onto the bed. "The right choice?" she mused, "Was there ever any doubt?"

Chapter 3
Tall Tales and Good-Night Kisses

Kelli slipped her hanger holding her favorite red dress on the clothes rod in the spacious walk-in closet. Tenderly, she caressed the smooth, silky fabric as it slipped through her fingers. "Why did I even bring this along?" she mused. "I'm not likely to attend many dressy parties up here!"

Carefully she closed the closet doors and wandered across the room to the large mirror suspended above the dresser. "You need that nap, Kelli Saunders," she said, studying the dark circles beneath her eyes. "But first, a warm, relaxing bath."

Absently, she shed her travel-weary clothes and slipped into the cuddly comfort of her pink hooded robe. "Hmm, let's see—soap, shampoo, conditioner."

Entering the cream-toned bathroom, Kelli sighed with pleasure. The thick, sumptuous carpet tickled her bare toes. She yawned and reached into the curtain-shrouded tub to turn on the shower control and the faucets. Hot water sprayed from the shower head. Before she could remove her hand from behind the curtain, something or someone jabbed the beige-and-peach shower curtain into her face.

"Yieek!" she screamed, jumping back in fright. Her breath came in short gasps as she watched the curtain jab out at her. Gathering her courage, Kelli threw the shower curtain wide open.

First a spray of warm water met her face; then a streak of green energy propelled itself up, over her head, and into the dark confines of the hood of her robe in an effort to escape the deluge.

Kelli screamed and gyrated wildly about the room while the yet unidentified object thrashed about, trying to escape her hysteria. The shower continued unabated.

While she failed to hear, six rushing feet sounded on the stairs.

"Miss Kelli! Miss Kelli! Are you all right?" Petey cried from the hallway, pounding on the door.

"Unlock the door, Miss Kelli!" Lisa called.

Kelli attempted to steady her fingers in order to unzip the robe and throw it to the floor. She watched in horror as a dazed, bug-eyed frog peered from beneath the pink heap and leaped over the toilet and into the wastebasket. Finally she realized that the water from her shower was still soaking the bathroom carpet. She quickly turned it off.

Linking her fingers together in an effort to control their shaking, she called out to her would-be rescuers. "I think I'm OK. I'll open the door in just a second." Cautiously she reached down, and with two fingers, lifted the offending garment. After inspecting it carefully from every angle, she shuddered, then put it on.

Once the robe was zipped safely to her neck, Kelli opened the door. Two pale, anxious faces stared up at her. The third smirked knowingly from the shadows.

"Benjamin! Where's Benjamin? You hurt my Benjamin!" Petey wailed, scooting past Kelli in an effort to locate his friend. "Oh, there you are, Benjamin. I'm sorry Miss Kelli scared you so." The boy and the frog eyed Kelli accusingly. "It won't happen again." Indignant, he sniffed and marched out of the room.

"Oh, I'm so sorry, Miss Kelli. I forgot to tell you that on warm days Petey often keeps Benjamin in the tub." The twinkle in Pamela's eyes belied her innocence.

"So that's how you want to play the game, is it?" Kelli breathed, a wry smile forming on one side of her mouth. "Well, no harm done. I used to own a pet frog myself. I called him Horatio. Benjamin just startled me. I'm sure I'll check more carefully before I shower again."

Uncertain as to whether or not she'd won the confrontation, Pamela tossed her nose into the air and tromped back down the stairs.

"I am sorry, Miss Kelli. I hope you aren't mad at us." Lisa's compassionate face looked up into hers.

From the foot of the stairs, Grandma Karpenko called, "Is everything all right up there? Are you OK, Miss Saunders? Do you need any help?"

"Grandma's not supposed to climb the stairs," Lisa confided. "She gets dizzy."

Kelli placed her arm on the girl's shoulder and walked to the landing. "Don't worry, Mrs. Karpenko, everything's just fine now. I'll need to sop up a little water, however."

The delayed shower finally taken, and clean-up from the earlier "frog-follies" completed, Kelli returned to her room to regroup her thoughts. Wrapping the homemade quilt about her, Kelli stretched out on the bed, consigning fidgety frogs, soggy carpets, and suspected pranks to the past, at least temporarily. She yawned and stretched, her mind drifting again southward to Oregon. She could almost smell the luscious aromas of her mother's hot apple pie and frying potatoes.

"M-m-m. I'm sure going to miss your great cooking, Mom," Kelli declared swiping a spicy potato wedge from the platter. "You make the best Jojos this side of the Mississippi."

"Hands off, young lady," Mother ordered, with a twinkle in her eye. "You can wait until mealtime, I'm sure. Supper will be ready in five minutes." The woman scraped the potatoes from a pan.

"I love you." Kelli came up behind her mother and gave her a squeeze. "Mom, how do you know for sure you're following the Lord's will? I'm not as confident as I first felt."

"That's good. You're wise enough to recognize your own weaknesses." The older woman paused. "I guess you have to learn to recognize His voice."

"Well, God hasn't come to me in a dream or spoken out of a thunderclap—or even in a still, small voice, for that matter," Kelli admitted.

"When Dad and I face a major decision, we weigh the pros and cons of each possibility, then present our observations to the Lord and ask Him to impress us with the right choice. After that, your Dad and I go to the Lord separately. Independent of each other, we usually come to the same decision; then we pray He will block it if it is not His will. Then we move out in faith."

"I can see how that works for you two, but I'm all alone," Kelli reminded. "There've been times when I knew the Lord's will for me, like waiting to marry Jeff. I guess I feel so alone right now."

"Kelli, claim the promise, 'In all they ways acknowledge him, and he shall direct they paths.'" Her mother paused, then added, "And remember, Dear, you aren't completely alone. God has something or someone special for you; just give Him time."

"Mother! Jeff *is* my someone special!"

Her mother's eyes glistened as she mumbled, "Perhaps."

Slowly Kelli returned to consciousness. Half awake, she scanned the unfamiliar room. Alaska! Not Oregon. She noticed the framed motto on her nightstand and sat up in order to read the words. "If you love something, set it free. If it never returns, it was not yours in the first place. If it returns, it is yours forever." She smiled, thinking of how Jeff had clung so tightly to her, that she'd felt stifled, pressured.

"Miss Kelli," Lisa called from beyond the bedroom door. "Miss Kelli, Grandma says to see if you're still asleep. Are you? If you are, I'm not to waken you."

Kelli chuckled. "I'm awake. Just a minute and I'll open the door."

After slipping into a skirt and blouse, Kelli opened the door, and Lisa stepped inside. "Oh, you look so pretty. I bet you have lots and lots of gorgeous dresses, hmmm? And lots and lots of boyfriends too!" Lisa's eyes sparkled as she watched Kelli brush her hair.

"Well, not too many of either, I'm afraid. While I finish fixing my hair, you may look at my dresses if you like. They're in the closet."

Embarrassed, Lisa drew back. "Oh, no! Grandma says I mustn't be nosy."

"Hey, I like looking at pretty clothes too. You'll show me yours later, so it's only fair, isn't it?" Kelli asked as she caught her long hair into an upsweep, fastening it with a tortoise comb.

A grin spread across the freckled face. "That sounds great, but I don't have too many, you know. I outgrew most of the ones I brought with me from California," Lisa said opening the closet. She carefully removed each dress and its hanger for a full, appreciative inspection. Lisa held her favorites up before her to view in the mirror.

"Oh, Miss Kelli! This red one is yummy!" Lisa pirouetted in a swirl of scarlet chiffon. "Daddy would love this. He's crazy about red dresses. Mamma wore one something like it the night they met. It was at a party in college. I've seen the picture."

Kelli's eyes misted as she watched the child's delight, remembering her own preteen dreams of parties, dashing heroes, and beautiful gowns.

"Lisa," a voice called from the bottom of the stairs, "did you call Miss Saunders?"

"Oh! I forgot!" Lisa replied, running into the hall. "I am sorry, Grandma, Miss Kelli and I've been talking. We'll be right down." Without waiting, Kelli and Lisa hurried downstairs and into the kitchen.

"Well, you certainly look pretty, Miss Saunders, and I bet a mite hungry too," Grandma Karpenko said, scraping the last of the corn into the bowl.

"Please call me Kelli. I'll feel much more at home that way," Kelli urged.

"OK, but only if you call me Grandma."

Kelli nodded approvingly. "That's a deal! By the way, I have two capable hands, as long as they're told what to do," she volunteered.

"Well, tonight everything's under control. Tomorrow I'll put you to work. You'll be sorry you made such an offer," the older woman added with a chuckle.

"That's why I'm here, remember, to make life easier for you."

"That's the excuse I gave Peter, I'll admit. Mainly, I want these children to have proper schooling, manners, and some Christian principles. They need these things badly. Don't get me wrong; my son is a good man. But he's still hurting over Liz's death, and he can't spend the time with the children they deserve. Meanwhile, they're growing up without anyone."

The woman ran her fingers through her short-cropped hair. "Till now, I've been able to supply some of their needs, but with my illness, I just don't have the strength anymore. But look at you, you're just bubbling over with youth and vitality."

Kelli laughed and replied, "Those assets I have. I just hope I possess all the other qualities and skills you desire."

"Hey, we're hungry!" Petey called, bounding into the room.

Grandma grabbed the serving dish and hurried to the table. "Patience, dear boy, patience," she reminded. Kelli followed.

After all were seated, Kelli bowed her head. The children look questioningly from Kelli to Grandma and back again. "They'll get used to it," she mused. "That's why they hired me."

Grandma eyed Kelli, then bowed her own head. "Children, close your eyes. Miss Kelli will offer the blessing."

Later during the meal, Grandma apologized. "I'm sorry that Peter isn't here to greet you. I thought he'd be home before now."

Pamela sighed with importance as she explained. "Yes, my father must ride the circuit to be sure each of the transceivers functions properly. Otherwise, the information recorded on his laboratory monitors will be faulty. Often, I go with him, but Grandmother needed me to help prepare for your arrival." Kelli detected a trace of resentment in Pamela's voice.

"I go too, sometimes!" Petey announced, biting into a slice of bread.

"You've only gone once, Petey. You are too young to be of any real help," Pamela snipped.

Sitting up as straight as possible, he turned toward his sister, "You—you think you're a real hot shot!"

"Petey! Where did you ever pick up that phrase?" Grandmother scolded.

Petey wilted. "Dad calls Uncle Roger that all the time," he defended.

Kelli smiled to herself watching the verbal ping pong match. "A challenge, that's what you have here," she decided.

After the supper dishes were done, Grandma, Kelli, and the children gathered around the fireplace in the living room. Lisa lead Kelli to the double-seated rocker. "Don't worry about Pamela; she's just getting too big for her britches."

Overhearing the remark, Petey's eyes lighted up, "She is? Grandma? If Pamela is getting too big for her britches, may I have her brand new Levi's?" Everyone except Pamela laughed.

"Brothers!" Pamela glowered and plopped down on an oversized pillow in front of the fireplace.

Lisa snuggled closer to her new teacher. "Do you have any brothers or sisters, Miss Kelli?" she asked.

"Yes, I have a big sister, Rhonda, and a new brother-in-law. She got married last summer. They live in California about 200 miles from my home in Oregon. I miss her a lot," Kelli admitted, staring into the glowing logs.

Lisa frowned. "I hope you won't miss her too much, Miss Kelli."

"Oh, I expect I'll enjoy my short stay in—"

"Miss Kelli, you might not," Pamela interrupted. "We have wolves, mountain lions, and grizzly bears too. They come down to the clearing sometimes." Dimples punctuated Pamela's face as she warmed to her subject. "They're quite dangerous, you know."

"No problem," Kelli assured her. "We have mountain lions in southern Oregon. And they say there are bears, but I never actually saw one."

"Oh, but our bears are bigger," Petey added. "The grizzly bear is as tall as a house."

Grandma patted the young boy's arm. "Now, Petey, that's a bit of an exaggeration. I believe they grow to seven or eight feet."

"Well," he defended, "that's still pretty tall, don't you think?"

"Sure do—wouldn't want to meet one. When I was younger, around your age, Petey, my family would visit my grandma's house in Idaho. My uncles and cousins would tell wild tales about the panthers and bears there. I'd get so scared I couldn't sleep."

Two hours and many tales later, Grandma suggested that the children should prepare for bed. With baths taken, all hugs and kisses appropriated, Kelli volunteered to tuck the three children in.

When Kelli approached Pamela's bed, the girl informed her, "I'm much too old to be tucked in, Miss Kelli."

"No one's too old to be loved, Pamela," Kelli reminded, then bent over and kissed her on the forehead.

"Good night, Miss Kelli," Lisa called from the other side of the room.

Kelli tiptoed to Lisa's side and kissed her soft cheek. "Good night, Honey. Thank you for making me feel at home."

A warm glow passed through Kelli as Lisa wrapped her arms around Kelli's neck and whispered, "I'm glad you came to us."

"Me too," Kelli admitted.

As she approached Petey's bedroom across the hall, the light through the open door illuminated his bed. At first he appeared to be asleep.

Tenderly, Kelli brushed a strand of hair from his forehead then kissed him.

"Good night, Petey," she whispered.

"Good night," he replied, grinning up at her. "Don't let the grizzlies getcha."

Chapter 4
Bears in the Night

Kelli tiptoed down the stairs to the living room, where Grandma Karpenko sat watching the flames in the fireplace.

"It's nice to have a few quiet minutes at the end of the day," Grandma admitted. "If you like to read, you should check out my son's library." She pointed toward the door at the base of the stairs. "It's a little lopsided in favor of the earth sciences, but perhaps you can find something that interests you. Please don't be offended if I retire early, but it's been a busy day for me."

"Oh no. Please don't stay awake on my account. I'm somewhat of a night owl. I might read awhile, though I am pretty sleepy tonight," Kelli said as she curled up on the sofa to enjoy the crackling fire. Grandma nodded and padded from the room.

Once alone, Kelli decided to check out the books in the library. Browsing past shelves of biographies, essays, and novels to the science textbooks, she chose volume two of the *Alaskan Travel Guide* and carried it to the oversized leather recliner by the window. She slipped past the pages of full-color photographs of salmon, halibut, and cod; of hemlock, spruce, and pine; of wolverine, fox, and caribou. She paused at the picture of the dreaded grizzly bear. Considering many of Alaska's remote and rugged mountain areas, Kelli assured herself that the bear, pictured towering over a six-foot-tall hunter, would not be an immediate threat to her security. Hours swept by until even the padded arm of the recliner felt uncomfortable. She twisted her stiffened shoulders in the confines of the chair, trying to locate a more comfortable spot.

Slowly, imperceptibly, the strange sensation of being watched crept over her. Thinking one of the children might have come looking for her, she glanced up from the book.

"An Alaskan grizzly!" she breathed unevenly, frozen at the sight of the huge creature standing in the doorway to the library. Within her mind, logic challenged her initial reaction. "Impossible! How could such an animal get into the house?"

In her misty world of semiconsciousness, an unreasonable panic cried, "Run stupid! Run!" Yet, try as she might, Kelli remained riveted to the chair cushion. Her brain again radioed the message, "Escape," but her legs refused to obey.

"I must be dreaming! If I pinch myself—" When she tried, her fingers grasped futilely at the air.

The creature approached slowly, stopping inches in front of where she sat. It reached down and touched her shoulder with its monstrous paw. This triggered her to action.

A blood-curdling, Twilight-Zone scream erupted from her throat, "A-a-a-EEEYOW!" She exploded from the chair and heaved the heavy travel guide into the beast's face.

"Hey, what's the matter with you? Are you crazy, Woman? You could kill a man with that!" The tall, dark-bearded man shielded himself from her attack. He raised his hand to the reddening bruise on his forehead as Kelli scrambled past and out of the room.

From beyond the open door, Kelli heard the man bellow, "You scared me half to death, Woman!"

Mortified at what she'd done, Kelli stopped halfway up the stairs and turned to face him standing at the foot of the stairs.

"I do hope that this is not a sample of what we might expect out of you while you're with us, Miss Saunders! You are Miss Saunders, I presume?"

Torn between embarrassment and shock, she replied, "Yes, I am Miss Saunders. And, yes, you can expect just such a reaction whenever you come creeping up on me in the middle of the night!"

The man laughed. "How would you have me announce myself, in my own home, I might add? With a brass band and twenty baton twirlers?" he teased. "I called out your name as soon as I noticed you asleep in my chair. I've walked through the room at least five times during the last fifteen minutes. And since I intend to go to bed presently, I thought you might find the guest room more comfortable." He raised one eyebrow mockingly.

"Oh," Kelli began. "I'm afraid I was dreaming. I thought you were a grizzly." She fluttered nervously down the stairs to inspect the damage she'd inflicted upon her employer's forehead. "I'm so embarrassed. Did I hurt you? Oh dear, perhaps you need some disinfectant and a band-aid."

"I'll be fine, I think. I realize I need a shave or at least a trim, but I didn't think I'd become that ferocious looking to be mistaken for a bear." Peter scratched at his two-week growth of beard. "I honestly didn't mean to startle you, Miss Saunders."

"No, it's my fault. I apologize for invading your domain, but your mother suggested I find a book to read. And, obviously, I found the wrong one."

Kelli turned at the sound of Pamela's voice from the top of the stairs. "Daddy, is that you?"

Kelli covered her eyes. "This is so embarrassing!" she whispered.

Peter's eyes twinkled at her discomfort. "Yes, Princess, I'm home," he answered. "Go back to bed. Miss Saunders and I are just getting acquainted."

"May I come downstairs and have a cup of cocoa with you?" the little girl pleaded.

"No ma'am! You hop back in bed. I have everything under control. I'll see you in the morning," he said, clapping his hands twice for emphasis. "Well, Miss Saunders, now that I'm wide awake, I demand that you do penance by whipping up a batch of hot cocoa."

"Do penance?" she whispered, her lips tilting into a grin. "If anyone is to do penance, it should be you for frightening me so. And, please, stop calling me Miss Saunders all the time. I feel like you're talking to my mother or my Aunt Terry."

A deep chuckle arose from his throat as he preceded Kelli to the kitchen. "What shall I call you then?"

"I answer to Kelli usually, though your children have decided to call me Miss Kelli." She hopped up onto the wooden counter stool. "And what shall I call you?"

He hauled a teakettle from the cupboard, filled it with hot tap water, and set it on a burner. "Peter, like *Peter and the Wolf*? Except this time it was a bear," he teased. "Nothing better at the end of the day than hot chocolate and chocolate-chip cookies. Help yourself." He stuffed a cookie into his mouth as he set the mushroom-shaped ceramic cookie jar in front of her. "After eating my own grub or Dr. Lee's bizarre concoctions for two weeks, I gorge myself on Mom's home cooking. But then, that's not your problem, since you are here to teach, not cook." As he talked the teakettle began to sing. He grabbed two mugs from the wall hooks behind the stove and filled them with boiling water, then added the powdered cocoa.

Kelli laughed as he handed her one of the cups. "Don't sell me short, Sir. I CAN cook! My meals might not be gourmet cuisine, but they're filling. I happen to be half Italian. And have you ever met an Italian woman, half or otherwise, who can't cook?" Kelli dipped her cookie into the steaming hot chocolate.

"I can see that you and my mother will get along famously. A

Russian cook and an Italian one, albeit half Italian. Maybe you're only half a cook?" He added, grinning insolently as he stole one of the cookies she'd placed on her saucer.

She started in surprise. "Well, I guess you'll never know, since I'm hired to teach," she taunted. "Seriously, what are my duties beyond the usual three R's?"

A frown clouded Peter's deep-brown eyes. "My mother believes the children are suffering from spiritual malnutrition. Personally, I'm not certain that's a bad thing. But Liz would have agreed with Mom, so I hired you. Oh, Liz was my wife; she died recently," he added hurriedly.

"It's been getting more and more difficult for my mother to keep up with the kids, with Petey especially. Pamela's been a big help, but she's a child and shouldn't be required to assume adult responsibilities." Peter stared past Kelli into the darkened living room, lost in a world of anxieties she couldn't yet understand.

"I guess I'm asking the impossible of such a young girl. I'd forgotten just how young twenty-two actually is until I saw you asleep in that chair." He held a cookie in the chocolate until it crumbled to the bottom of the cup. "Mother expects you to teach morals, manners, and scholastics. She'd appreciate it if you'd be a surrogate parent. And probably lurking somewhere in the dark recesses of her mind, she hopes you'll lasso me into marriage. Mother firmly believes, 'it is not good that man should live alone'—especially her son. But we'll disappoint her in that score, Miss Kelli. I'm not interested in taking on a junior miss or any other woman as a wife."

Shocked at his directness, Kelli sat speechless, alternately bristling and gulping in surprise, "I . . . I . . . !" She knew her face revealed the thoughts racing through her mind, but nothing had prepared her for Peter's accusation.

"That was rather clumsy of me, wasn't it?" He scowled.

"Yes," she replied simply.

"It's nothing personal, mind you. For that matter, it has nothing to do with you. I'm sure there are any number of appropriate young men here in the wilds of Alaska ready to hop into your pretty noose," he added.

"Sir, I am afraid you are operating under a number of misconceptions. I am twenty-two years old, though not ready for the geriatric set, to be sure, but also not fresh out of pinafores and knee socks," Kelli sputtered.

"Barely," he mumbled.

"I am also a legally registered voter, a college graduate qualified to teach in any elementary school in the United States and Canada, whether the curriculum be morals, academics, or manners." Under her breath, Kelli added, "Perhaps your children are not the only ones who need lessons in the last area."

"You've got this all wrong—" he began.

"Look, I applaud your honesty. But I didn't come to Alaska to find a husband. I have a perfectly adequate specimen studying medicine back East in Maryland. So rest assured, your gynephobia is safe around me."

Peter attempted to explain, "I just wanted everything clearly understood between us."

"As it should be, Dr. Karpenko. I can't control my age, but I believe you will find my skills satisfactory. If not, feel free to send me packing," Kelli added, praying that he wouldn't take her offer seriously. "I'm not a quitter. I finish what I start, and I'd like the chance to do so in this situation. But if I am totally repulsive to you or appear flippant or irresponsible, or if you think I'll harm your children in any way, then by all means, I will leave tomorrow." Kelli's hands shook as she brushed stray cookie crumbs off the table into a paper napkin.

"Hey, hey, hey! Who said anything about leaving? I think we're both overreacting here. I should have kept my opinions about your age to myself, along with my remarks about your love life. In other words, I blew it. Will you accept my apology?" he asked, arching one eyebrow questioningly. "Do you think we could possibly start over?"

Kelli managed a tight little smile. "Perhaps we should," she admitted.

"Good, and I'll admit that maybe mom was right in bringing you here," he added. "It's just that you are so young. . . ."

She ran the dishcloth across the table's surface. "A strange thing, maturity. I've learned it has less to do with one's looks than with one's attitude."

"Touché" he drawled, as he got up from the table and strolled from the room.

Kelli stood staring at the sink for several seconds. "I can't believe it," she mused, shaking her head in wonder. "In one breath, he makes me laugh; in the very next, he rankles me."

Suddenly the whole situation became humorous. "What a bizarre night! First I heave a book at my employer's forehead; then I'm considered a femme fatale—a bubble-gum-totin' femme fatale at that! This has to be a first for me." Kelli chuckled to herself as she headed up the stairs to her room.

Chapter 5
A Thorn in the Flesh

Goosebumps dotted Kelli's flesh as she hopped from beneath the warm covers into the cool bedroom air. Unused to the partial all-night light of Alaskan summers, she had awakened early and stood by her bed shivering. "It must take time to adjust to the colder climate," she decided.

From her window, she viewed the dense evergreen forest climbing the mountain behind the cabin. In so many ways it reminded her of Oregon. She settled into the rocker for her morning devotions. Kelli read from her Bible for a time, then knelt to pray.

"Father, You know much better than I what problems I will encounter today. And You already have the solutions in hand. Please help me to remember that and to listen when You try to guide me. Amen."

Her thoughts turned to Grandma Karpenko. Whether anyone admitted it or not, Kelli could see that the woman was seriously ill. One glance and Kelli knew she'd be needed far beyond her tutorial duties.

Whipping through her shower and dressing, Kelli was downstairs and ready to work in record time. "Hi there. Tell me where everything is and I'll help," she called, bounding into the sunlit kitchen.

"That's quite all right, Miss Kelli," Pamela announced. "I am quite capable of preparing breakfast for the family. And I can do it more efficiently alone, thank you." The younger girl set the pancake turner down on the counter.

Kelli smiled at the young girl's defense of her territorial rights. "You know, I think you're right. Making breakfast might be just the task for you. OK, that's your assignment. You'll make breakfasts." Kelli paused to appreciate the look of confusion on Pamela's face. "Now, I wonder what Lisa enjoys doing most? I've found we usually do our best when we enjoy the task." Kelli smiled sweetly and reached into the cupboard where she'd seen Grandma put the brown, quilted placemats the evening before. "I'll set the table while you finish the eggs."

Without a word, Pamela sizzled more than the eggs, while Kelli continued talking as if nothing were wrong. "I think your grandmother needs our help more than she lets on. She'll feel better knowing everything is running smoothly. Don't you agree?"

"Are you talking to yourself, Miss Kelli?" Lisa asked upon entering the room.

"Oh no, Pamela's making breakfast, and I'm setting the table." Kelli filled the breakfast glasses with ice-cold orange juice. "Now tell me what chores you'd like to do, Lisa." Kelli asked innocently.

"I'd like to learn to cook, but Pamela always gets to do that. So, I guess I'm stuck with the dishes," Lisa sighed.

"Oh, I don't know. You could do lunch. We could find a bunch of yummy recipes to try." Kelli smiled as Lisa's eyes gleamed with delight.

Kelli continued, "Petey and I can do the breakfast dishes, Pamela and I—the lunch dishes. And you and I can clean up after supper. How's that?" Kelli noted the silence coming from the other half of the kitchen.

"I don't know. Pamela never has to do dishes. And besides, supper's the biggest meal," she reminded.

"Right, giving us more time to enjoy one another's company. I could teach you some of the games my sister and I used to play while washing the family dishes. Of course, I'll have to talk with Grandma first to be sure that she approves of our plans," Kelli said, darting another glance at the stone-faced Pamela.

"Daddy came home last night," Pamela announced, eyeing Kelli malevolently. "I'll call him." At Pamela's announcement, Lisa and Petey squealed and ran from the kitchen to find him.

Kelli listened to the chatter as the three children led their father to the table. It was obvious that these children missed their father dearly whenever he was gone, and it was equally apparent that he missed them too.

They soon returned to the kitchen with Lisa hanging on his right arm and Petey perched in the crook of his left.

"Well, good morning. How is the intrepid Miss Kelly this lovely morning?" a clean-shaven Peter asked, as he placed his son in a chair. "Where's Grandma?"

He listened as Pamela told him about Grandma's excruciating headache.

"Guess what Miss Kelli promised this morning? She said we all get to help make meals while Grandma is sick. We're going to divide them up. Isn't that neat?" Lisa bubbled between mouthfuls of toast and scrambled eggs.

"She did, did she?" He nodded congenially toward Kelli. "And what else has Miss Kelli done?"

It was the wrong question. Petey immediately launched into a complete report of Benjamin and the bathtub, every embarrassing detail. Tears ran down Peter's face as he laughed at his son's graphic description of the catastrophe. Even Kelly laughed, in spite of her discomfort.

The light banter continued throughout the meal. When he'd finished the last of his scrambled eggs, Peter glanced warmly toward Kelli. "I appreciate your taking up the slack for my mother, Miss Kelli." He leaned back in the chair and placed the crumpled napkin beside his empty plate. "It sounds like you've made quite a hit already," he taunted.

"I'm working on it." Kelli blushed, her eyes flickered toward Pamela, who suddenly found her eggs extremely interesting.

After cleaning the kitchen, Kelli and the children gathered in the large classroom. The twins collected their school books in order to show their teacher what they'd been doing.

"Now, first things first. We need a daily and a weekly schedule. Then I need a list of your favorite foods and your favorite classes. We'll include home economics as part of your curriculum, so you'll be graded on how well things turn out in the kitchen."

Petey tugged at Kelli's sleeve. "Me too?" he asked.

"Absolutely!" Kelli tousled his hair. "Now, let me see, what have you girls been doing in your schoolwork?"

Once a routine was established, the weeks flew by quickly. When home, Peter enjoyed teasing the children about their cooking. Before long, he measured the success of a casserole or a pot of homemade soup by appropriate letter grades. The children thrilled at his approval. Kelli watched and listened, appreciating the children's happiness.

Kelli enjoyed the twin's outstanding scholastic achievements in spite of the fact that they'd been isolated from other children for so long. Petey insisted on doing his fair share of "schoolwork" too. Other habits became a part of their daily pattern, such as offering the blessing at mealtimes and praying before going to sleep at night.

Though complimenting Kelli on the children's academic achievements, Peter never commented on his children's new prayer life. Kelli did notice that whenever he was home, he managed to be in the living room when she gathered the children together for family worship, under the guise of evening story time. It wasn't long, though, before Peter joined the circle as each child reported his daily concerns to the new Unseen Friend. Occasionally, when Grandma felt up to it, she joined the circle too.

One evening, after the last child had been tucked in bed, Kelli wrapped a hand-crocheted shawl about her shoulders and walked to the lake. She'd grown to love the clear Alaskan sunsets and hated to miss even one. She sat down on a log, draped the shawl across her knees, and stared out across the surface of the water. Engrossed in recalling the day's events, she failed to hear the approaching footsteps.

"Beautiful, isn't it?" Peter said softly. Surprised, Kelli looked up, unconsciously brushing one hand through her hair.

"Oh, you startled me. I guess I was lost in thought. Unfamiliar territory, you know," she replied as she returned her attention to the lake.

"Hardly. You're the most intelligent, organized, and creative young woman I've ever met. I'm impressed with what you've accomplished here." He tossed a small piece of bark into the water.

"Well . . . thank you," she gulped, unnerved by the unsolicited compliments.

"I've never seen the children so obedient, polite, and most of all, happy. Not since—" Peter stopped midsentence, then straddled the log and sat down. Silently they watched the constantly changing light show in the western sky.

"I appreciate your saying so," she began. "I know you weren't too thrilled about hiring me at first, so your compliments mean even more. My mom always said that children usually appear happier if their lives are somewhat structured. I guess we all need to know we're loved and that our efforts are appreciated." Kelli stretched her long, slim legs out in front of her, crossing them at the ankles.

Slowly, as if studying the log's bark under one of his microscopes, Peter continued. "Also, I've come to appreciate the religious portion of your curriculum too. It brings back memories—good ones. And I've noticed that the kids don't squabble so much. Even Pamela seems to be adjusting. She was very close to her mother, you know." He picked up a short stick and scribbled abstract designs in the sand.

"My conversations with God are not really a part of my curriculum. He's very much a part of my life. And, yes, Pamela is softening. She must have been hurt badly," Kelli answered softly, studying the shadows filling the valley. "You know, I never would have had the courage to come to Alaska if I weren't sure God was leading."

"Why did you come?" he asked. His eyes remained shaded, making it impossible for Kelli to read his expression.

"Well, first, I believe that the Lord pointed me north. Why, I'm not sure. I'd planned to marry Jeff. He's the one I told you about, studying at Johns Hopkins University." She paused, then continued, "I don't know. Maybe Alaska was a way out of getting married right then. So many of my friends are married and having problems already. I know one thing. As far as I'm concerned, my marriage will be for keeps."

Peter glanced over at Kelli and nodded. "That's good," he said. "So many people today look at marriage as a game or at best an open-ended contract. If you have doubts, it's better to face them before you take that final step."

"I don't know whose love I doubted the most, Jeff's or mine. I had a teaching job lined up for next fall at a preppy girls' school in Connecticut. I felt very lucky to have it since most of my fellow elementary education majors couldn't find anything in their field."

"Then, what happened?" He urged.

"Well, the retiring teacher decided to stay on another year, so my appointment was postponed," she explained. "When your mother's letter arrived, Miss Andrews, the college's placement officer, thought of me—and here I am."

His brows knitted with concern. "You're quite young to be so certain of everything. How do your parents feel about your being here?"

"Dr. Karpenko, I've been young all my life. My folks are used to it. And fortunately, they recognize that I'm an adult now, capable of making my own decisions, even if you are not inclined to agree with them," she added. "You know, when I hear you talk over your ham radio, it makes me just a little homesick. My dad's a ham operator—WB7UZN."

"Really?" he asked. "We should set up a weekly schedule for you to talk with them, at least when I'm here."

"That would be nice," Kelli admitted, as she wiggled her sandaled foot further into the sand mound building at her feet. "Ouch!" she gasped.

"What happened? Let me see," Peter demanded, taking her injured foot into his hands. The twilight made it difficult for him to examine the injury. "Hmm, you managed to get a thorn beneath your big toenail."

Kelli winced as he touched the thorn with his thumb.

She attempted to pull her foot from his grasp. "I can manage."

"No way. Remember how you fussed about my forehead the night you clobbered me with my own book? Now it's my turn, young lady. We'd better get you to the house and get disinfectant on it right away." Peter stood, reached down, and lifted her to her feet. "Can you walk on it?"

"I think so," she gulped, gingerly stepping down.

"I'd better help you," he suggested, slipping his arm around her waist. "Put your arm around my neck and lean on me."

After a painful trip back to the house, Peter led Kelli to the living room couch. "You sit here while I get the first-aid kit," he ordered as he disappeared into the kitchen.

When he returned, he had enough medical supplies to treat a division of wounded GI's. She giggled at the solemn expression on his face as he carefully dabbed a wet cloth around the puncture wound. Her laughter changed to a grimace when he yanked the thorn from her toe.

"It looks like it all came out," he mumbled as he examined the thorn in the light from the table lamp. "I'll just put some of this antiseptic cream on your toe, and you should be fine."

Kelli leaned back against the couch and closed her eyes momentarily as he applied the cream. When she opened them, she was surprised to find him gazing at her. She smiled questioningly.

"I guess that will take care of everything," he said, as he stuffed the first-aid equipment back in the case. "If you experience any discomfort in the next few days, let me know."

"Yes, Dr. Karpenko," Kelli teased.

He flashed a smile and winked. "Don't be impertinent, young lady!"

Chapter 6
The Picnic

Kelli's fingers rambled across the piano keys, producing a recital piece she'd memorized as a child. She gazed out at the early-morning mist rising off the lake. So much had changed during the short time she'd been in Alaska. She'd arrived feeling confident, certain of her goals and expectations. And as a teacher, Kelli still felt assured her charges were getting the best education she could give. However, within her personal life, she felt confused.

What do I want besides teaching? she mused. Is Jeff part of my answer? She wasn't sure. Instead of lessening as time passed, her uncertainties seemed to grow.

The children. Ah, the children. Kelli smiled tenderly. Besides math and English and all the required lessons, she'd enjoyed teaching Lisa all the precious little secrets usually shared between a mother and daughter—things like nail care, hair styling, and growing up. Occasionally, she wondered if Peter resented Lisa's obvious desire to imitate her.

Kelli frowned when she thought of Pamela, who spent most of her time fluctuating between affection and obstinacy. One minute she wants me to teach her how to hem a skirt, and the next, Kelli thought, she's putting hand lotion into my shampoo bottle.

Roaring like a locomotive, Petey rumbled past the window on his tricycle. The wheels rumbled over the wooden deck, making a terrible racket. When he spotted Kelli, he waved. She waved back.

"How will I ever say goodbye to that kid when I head back to the lower forty-eight?" she wondered. "In a matter of minutes, he stole my heart." His unlimited imagination allowed him to be everything from a bush pilot to a mountain climber. He played as rough and tough as any boy could, yet at night his warm, loving arms encircled Kelli's neck. And always, he'd plant a big, sloppy kiss on her cheek before snuggling down to sleep. Some nights he'd have nightmares and cry out for her. Kelli secretly enjoyed scurrying to his bedside, holding him in her arms, and rocking him back to sleep.

Then there was Mrs. Karpenko. Even to Kelli's untrained eyes, Grandma's pain appeared to be worsening. Grandma often mentioned her desire to return to her former family doctor in Boston, Massachusetts.

Kelli glanced toward the library door and thought of Peter. He was gone so often. She knew the children missed him desperately. And if the truth were to be known, she missed him as well. She missed the stimulating discussions they would have over anything from politics to the morality of euthanasia. She especially enjoyed learning about his research.

"I check substations while Dr. Lee holds a free clinic in each village," Peter explained. "It works out well for both of us. It would be mighty lonely otherwise, and dangerous for either of us to travel alone out there in the backcountry."

Kelli snapped awake at the thought of Peter. "You, young lady, are getting yourself too involved in this family's drama. You must remain more objective," she scolded. "After all, less than a year from now your Alaskan interlude will be over."

Kelli's mind wandered to Jeff, but since she had not heard from him in some time, his memory seemed fuzzy. Then it returned to Alaska. "I wonder if Dr. Lee is Roger Lee's father, or perhaps his brother?"

"Kelli," Grandma called from the library. "Roger just radioed in on the ham set to tell you to get ready for a hike and a picnic tomorrow. Peter and Dr. Lee will be coming in late tonight, to make it a foursome. And he said, 'Don't argue.'"

Kelli scowled, remembering all she had planned for the following day. "But, I—" she began.

"Really, Kelli," Grandma interrupted as she entered the living room, "when we hired you, we didn't intend to make you our prisoner. You do need time off, away from the children. Now, everything's arranged." She patted the young woman on the shoulder.

"But I can't leave you alone. I have lessons planned for the children, and we were scheduled to—"

"Oh pshaw! They'll wait. The children and I will do just fine. The twins will help me here in the house, so don't worry. Maybe we'll make a batch of brownies or something. Sometimes you're too conscientious!" Grandma insisted. "Now don't worry about a thing. You don't even have to fix lunch. Roger is bringing it. But, I bet neither he nor Peter would mind if you made some of your delicious berry turnovers for dessert," she remarked and bustled back to her apartment.

"OK, I'd better pick a few berries then. How did he know about my baking?" Kelli called.

"Perhaps Peter mentioned it," the woman replied.

When Petey and Pamela heard of the proposed picnic, they pouted throughout supper. Lisa, however, bubbled with excitement, repeating over and over how handsome Roger Lee was and what a great husband he'd make for Kelli.

"Now no matchmaking, Young Lady," Kelli scolded. Lisa just grinned mischievously.

Not knowing how rigorous the hike might be, Kelli went to bed earlier than usual that evening even though Peter would be home soon. Being a natural-born night owl, Kelli often greeted him on his arrival home. They had developed a habit of sharing hot chocolate and cookies late at night. This gave her time to bring him up to date on the children's progress, or at least that's what she told herself was the reason for their late-night talks.

He often spoke of his wife, Liz. Occasionally, Kelli would mention a few things about Jeff, but whenever she'd try to speak about God's guidance, Peter was anxious to change the subject.

With the children bedded for the night, Kelli discovered that sleep came quickly for her too.

"Miss Kelli?" A timid knock on her bedroom door brought her back to consciousness. "Miss Kelli?"

At first she thought it was Petey. Then she realized the voice was much too low. "Are you awake? The Lees will be here in forty-five minutes," Peter whispered. "Can you hear me?"

She shook her head, trying to clear the sleep from her brain. "OK, I hear you. What time is it?"

"It's four-fifteen. Are you sure you're awake?" He questioned again.

"Four-fifteen in the morning? Are you crazy? Better yet, am *I* crazy?" She mumbled, fumbling for the switch on the lamp beside her bed.

Tantalizing aromas drifted up the stairwell as she showered and blow-dried her hair. "Hmm," she thought, "pancakes certainly are an effective lure this morning." Catching her sleek, shoulder-length hair into a ponytail, she slipped a petal-pink T-shirt over her head and pulled on her most comfortable pair of jeans. A touch of perfume and a navy windbreaker completed her hiking outfit. Once ready, she tiptoed down the stairs to the kitchen.

"Hey there! You ready for our adventure?" Peter stood over the griddle, flipping flapjacks into the air like a seasoned chef.

"I'm not too sure. I've never done much hiking," she admitted, as she opened the refrigerator to find the pitcher of orange juice she'd prepared before going to bed.

"I promise we won't do any tricky climbing, not with a novice along," Peter assured her.

"That suits me just fine." She reached for the juice glasses on the cupboard shelf.

He placed two steaming hotcakes on one of the plates. "Besides, I think Roger may have planned this picnic for more reasons than a strenuous hike in the backcountry."

"And what is that supposed to mean?" Kelli eyed him suspiciously.

"Eat your breakfast before it gets cold," he ordered, slapping a square of butter atop the two pancakes.

"Come on, you can't make a statement like that and then drop the subject," she demanded.

"Oh, I don't know," Peter brought his plate of pancakes to the table and sat down, "just something his sister said."

Startled, Kelli looked up from her plate. "Sister? I didn't know he had a sister."

"Well, who do you think Dr. Lee is? She's his sister and the reason he came to Alaska in the first place. She's our local 'medicine man,' while he runs the only trading post for a radius of seventy-five miles," Peter explained, burning his tongue on the hot chocolate.

"I didn't realize Dr. Lee was female," Kelli replied, idly stirring her cocoa with her teaspoon.

Peter nursed his sore tongue with a corner of his paper napkin. "Suzanne is quite female!" he admitted.

When Peter spotted the Lees' plane coming in for a landing, he grabbed the small basket holding Kelli's berry turnovers and ran for the airstrip. She followed as best she could. Upon reaching the plane, Peter lifted her into the cockpit and made the appropriate introductions.

A tall, slim, platinum blonde with an open, friendly smile greeted her. "I've been so anxious to meet you, Kelli. Both Roger and Peter have told me so much about you. And from what I see, they were 100 percent correct in their evaluations."

Kelli smiled back and blushed. "Thank you, I think. I've heard quite a bit about you too," she answered.

Suzanne helped Kelli hunt for her seat-belt strap. Regardless of her relationship with Dr. Peter Karpenko, Kelli knew immediately that she and Suzanne Lee would become friends.

"Hey, didn't I tell ya', Sis?" Roger interrupted. "But, Old Buddy," he turned toward Peter, "I did find her first."

"Perhaps you've forgotten, I'm the one who originally brought her to Alaska," Peter joked good-naturedly.

"You men are embarrassing this poor girl to tears!" Suzanne scolded. "For today, she's with me. We gals have to stick together just to survive."

The six-seater plane climbed up over the lake, forming a wide arc toward the north. "And now for a geography lesson," Roger instructed. "*Alákshak* the Aleut Indian word for *peninsula,* or Alaska, is the largest state, double the size of Texas and fiftieth in population. It's the most northern and most western state."

"Wait a minute," Kelli interrupted. "What about Hawaii?"

"I was hoping the beautiful lady would ask that. The Aleutian Islands are farther west than Hawaii. And Juneau, our capital, is the same latitude as Stockholm, Sweden. Now, aren't you impressed?"

"Suitably," Kelli answered, "but may I be so bold as to ask where we are going?"

"You may," Peter answered, but said no more.

"Well, where are we going?"

"I was waiting for you to ask," he teased. "I thought you might enjoy climbing Mount McKinley."

Kelli gasped in horror. "What? No way! Peter, you said—"

Suzanne laughed and patted Kelli's arm. "He's kidding, Kelli. We're going to fly to Denali National Park and rent a Jeep to tour the area. It's magnificent close up."

Peter remained outside the banter, staring out the side window at the forest below. Kelli noticed, but said nothing.

"Did you know that the furthermost tip of the Aleutian Islands is only thirty miles from Siberia?" Roger rambled on with his travelogue throughout the rest of the flight. When they landed, a rental Jeep was waiting for them at the airstrip. Again, with the men seated in front and the women in back, they set off for their day in the wilds.

Hours later, after driving over the rough, back roads of the park, the four adventurers found a secluded spot where they could eat lunch.

"You gals grab the blankets, and we'll get the food. Do you think we have enough?" Roger lifted one of the baskets from the back of the Jeep, then another.

Suzanne poked her brother in the ribs. "The three of us will do fine," she teased, "but what will you eat?" He growled in mock anger.

They walked a short distance to a grassy clearing, and after spreading the blankets on the ground, the four dug into the food.

"Great food, Roger." Kelli reached for a second egg-salad sandwich. "I could stay here forever."

"Only until September, I'm afraid," Peter drawled. "Summertime temperatures are merely guests in these parts."

After angling for the last turnover, Roger stood up and stretched. "I feel the need for a hike to the lake. The sign by the road said it's only two miles from here."

Suzanne jumped to her feet, dusting the pastry crumbs from her jeans. "Sounds like just what the doctor ordered. I'd like to go."

"Kelli and I will wait here until you return," Peter announced before Kelli could voice her vote.

"Oh?" Suzanne uttered questioningly. "Well, OK. See you in a couple of hours, I guess." Suzanne left the startled Roger standing by the empty lunch baskets. "I'll beat you to the trail base, Little Brother."

Roger's face registered confusion. He wasn't quite sure what had happened to change his plans, but changed they certainly were.

"Hurry up, Slowpoke," Suzanne called as she broke into a brisk run.

"I guess I'll see you two later. Take care of her for me, Peter," he warned half jokingly, as he ran after his sister.

Feeling put out over Peter's cavalier attitude, Kelli scolded, "I could have hiked a two-mile trail. I'm not that out of shape, you know."

"I know," he said, drawing an envelope out of his pocket.

"Here. This is for you. I know you've been waiting a long time for it to arrive, and I wanted to give you some privacy while you read it." He knelt beside the basket and began packing the empty containers into it.

"Oh! Jeff! I thought he'd never write. Of course, I know how busy he must be settling into the medical program at the university." She mumbled aloud while Peter carried the two heavy baskets back to the Jeep.

As she read the long-awaited communique, her eyes darkened and pain contorted her face. She felt pale and dizzy, but continued to read.

Dear Kelli,

I don't know how to tell you, except to just come right out and say it. I've met a wonderful girl here at the university. She's everything I want in a woman.
She wants nothing more in her life than to be my wife (and can you believe it?), to wait on me hand and foot. I admit, I like it.
That was the one problem you and I had, if you remember right. You chose to go traipsing off to Alaska rather than marrying me. You had to do your own thing. Maybe things would have been different. . . .
Anyway, that's neither here nor there now. My folks have agreed to support us while I'm in school, so Sheila won't have to work. You'd like her.
I'm sorry. I never meant to hurt you. I hope you find everything you're looking for also.
Sincerely,

Jeff

Kelli bit her lip and vowed, "I won't cry, I won't." She buried her face into the warm, sunlit blanket. Her life had been planned, down to the last detail. Now what? she wondered. Immediately, she turned to her lifelong Comforter.

"How could this happen, Lord? How could Jeff do this?" She grasped her head in her hands. "Father, help me. I know You've promised to take care of me, and all I need to do is trust. But right now, I feel so confused."

A gentle hand on her shoulder reminded her that she wasn't alone. "May I help?" Peter asked, handing her a box of tissues.

Kelli swiped at her tears and look up into what seemed to her to be the most understanding eyes she'd ever encountered. "You knew, didn't you?" she sniffed, struggling to regain her composure.

"Yes, I guess so. He took so long to write—a man in love isn't that patient. He wouldn't risk losing you by letting so much time elapse between contact. When the letter came, I was afraid it carried bad news."

She yanked another tissue from the box and blew her nose. "He's marrying someone else, a Sheila somebody."

"It hurts to lose the one you love," he said, as if lost in his own memories. "When I lost Liz, I thought I would die, but, unfortunately, I didn't."

His words surprised her. "Don't say that! Don't ever say that! Life is a gift from God. Never wish it away," Kelli scolded. "Besides, those beautiful children of yours need you so much."

"I know that now. The way they're blossoming under your attention shows me that." With one finger, he lifted her chin, forcing her to look into his eyes. "But enough about me. How about you? What do you plan to do?"

The shock of his gentle touch unnerved her. "I wish I could go home," she sniffed.

"What? The brave, undaunted Kelli Saunders, who told me only a month ago that once she started something, nothing could make her quit?" A dimple in his right cheek teased at the corner of his mouth. "The one who said her life rests in the Lord? Has He suddenly changed His mind about your appointment? Is it only a fair-weather religion you preach?"

"No," Kelli defended, "He does take care of me, even through experiences like this. Of course I won't quit. It's just that whenever I got a stomachache or cut my knee or broke up with a boyfriend, home is where I longed to be," Kelli confessed reluctantly between the tears. "But I guess I'm not a little girl any more, huh?"

He removed another tissue from the box and gently wiped a stray tear from her cheek. "Thank heavens for that," he mumbled tersely, then stretched out on the grass to enjoy the sunshine, leaving Kelli to her own jumbled thoughts.

Chapter 7
Call in the Night

Grandma's headaches grew worse every day until the woman could barely lift her head without experiencing excruciating pain. Kelli concocted all sorts of activities to keep the children from disturbing her and anxiously awaited Peter's return from the backcountry. He'd been gone for more than a week, and now, with Grandma Karpenko taking a turn for the worse, Kelli was worried.

The minute Kelli spotted Peter's plane landing, she ran down the path to the airstrip. She reached him just as he was carrying some boxes into the storage shed. She picked up two of the lighter ones and headed toward the shed.

"Peter, I'm so glad you're here," Kelli called.

At the sound of her voice, Peter stepped out from inside the shed and asked, "Well, hello there. I didn't see you coming. What's wrong?" he asked, as he took the cartons from her hands and stepped back inside the shed.

She followed him. "Your mother needs you. She's in a lot of pain," Kelli warned.

The tiny shed was filled with all sizes and shapes of cardboard boxes, most of them were imprinted with brand names she recognized as electronic equipment. She shivered at the dampness inside the building.

"Here, let me help you stack the rest of these boxes," she volunteered. Together they unloaded the rest of the cartons and placed them inside the shed. As they walked to the house, Kelli explained all that had happened since he'd left.

When they entered Grandma's room, Peter hurried to his mother's side. Kelli waited near the doorway. When she saw him, she said, "Son, I'm afraid it's time for me to go into Anchorage, where medical help is more accessible. Suzanne is an excellent physician, but I think I need tests that she can't administer out here. I could get a small apartment for the winter months, though I'd still prefer Boston Medical Center and Dr. Vincent's help. He's tops in neurosurgery."

Peter sat on the edge of the bed, holding his mother's hand. "If you really want to fly to Boston, I won't stop you. I just wish you'd have the tests done in Anchorage. Then, if nothing improves, you could fly to Boston come spring."

Tears glistened in Kelli's eyes as she observed how gentle Peter was with his mother. She could readily imagine how compassionate he must have been with his dying wife. She could only guess at the loneliness he must carry. She felt helpless. She longed to ease Grandma Karpenko's pain also. But again, she realized her limitations.

Kelli carried an empty tumbler to the kitchen. For a time, she leaned against the kitchen counter, thinking. As she thought of how she'd come to love the older woman and how much she'd miss her, tears ran, unbidden, down Kelli's cheeks.

Footsteps approached from behind. "Are you crying for Grandma?" a tiny voice whispered.

"What? Oh, Lisa, you startled me. I didn't hear you coming," Kelli said, swallowing back her tears.

"Is Grandma going to die, like Mommy did? Pamela says she is." Lisa hesitated, as if saying it might make it happen.

Kelli wrapped her arms around the little girl. "I don't know, Sweetheart. Only God knows." Suddenly Kelli recognized that here was someone she could help; here was where she was needed. "Hey, why don't we go up to the classroom and make Grandma a supersized get-well card."

The girl nodded reluctantly. "I guess so," she said.

Kelli kissed the worried child on the cheek.

Bursting into tears, Lisa squeezed Kelli. "I hope I never lose you," she cried.

"Nor I you, Honey," Kelli replied, barely able to speak. "We'll be friends for ever and ever."

Without warning, like the startling sensation of being awakened while sleepwalking, Kelli panicked. "How will I feel next May, when it's time to leave?" she thought. An unexpected sadness engulfed her as she made her way to the stairs.

Lisa's artwork was a success. Before long, Petey had made a get-well card of his own. Even Pamela finished off a picture of a field of daisies with Get Well written across the bottom. Grandma praised them all fondly.

After dinner, Kelli snuggled down beneath the puffy quilt in her room, wanting only to sleep her troubles away, at least for a few hours.

"Miss Kelli? Miss Kelli, are you asleep?" Lisa's familiar voice called to her through the closed door.

"I'm not now," she thought. "Just a minute, Lisa." Reluctantly, she lifted her exhausted body out of the warm bed, wrapped her robe loosely about her, and opened the door.

"I'm sorry to wake you, but Daddy told me to ask you to come down to the library. He needs to talk with you," Lisa said, giving Kelli a quick squeeze around her waist. Kelli hugged her back and sent Lisa on her way.

She stepped back into her room and slipped into her fuzzy, pink slippers, ran her brush through her disarrayed curls, and hurried downstairs.

When she reached the library door, she paused and took a deep breath. "You rang?" she called, stepping into the book-lined room.

Peter stood staring out of the library window. His shoulders sagged. When he turned to face her, she noted the dark circles outlining his deep brown eyes. "I'm sorry, Kelli. I realize that you were probably asleep already, but what I have to say cannot wait," he said, motioning for her to sit down in the leather chair in front of his desk.

He walked to the shelf which housed his ham radio station. "First, I believe you said that you know how to operate a ham radio."

"Yes. Why?" she questioned.

"I realize it would be illegal for you to operate the system in my absence, but in an emergency it should be all right. I taught my mother how to work it, and Pamela knows how also. I'd like to teach you. Come here. I'd like to point out the idiosyncrasies of this setup."

"OK. But why?" Kelli asked.

"There's a storm in the area and it has turned north. So in approximately fifteen minutes, I am flying my mother to Anchorage. I've notified Roger. He'll monitor this frequency twenty-four hours a day, until I return. Now, if you need to contact him, use my call letters. They're right here on the wall, KL7AOP. His are KL7BRR. Try it."

"Look, I honestly do know how." Kelli fidgeted, tightening the tie on her pink robe.

"Please, I must be sure you know what to do before I leave," he said.

On her first call, Roger's teasing voice came back over the

receiver. "Hi there, KL7AOP. My, how your voice has changed. I like the improvement. It looks like I'll be your lifeline to the outside world for the next few days. Treat me nicely now," he added with a deep chuckle, then signed off.

Peter began sorting through some papers on his desk. "As soon as I get Mother settled in, I'll return. I'll be picking up a few supplies too. It will be inconvenient having everyone in Anchorage, but it can't be helped."

Kelli shook her head in disbelief. "Hey, wait a minute. Back up. You're taking us where?"

"To Anchorage, of course," he answered. "You don't think I'd leave you alone up here with three children for any length of time, do you?"

"I don't see why not. Why should the children's routine be changed? Other than visiting your mom, which the children couldn't do anyway, I see no reason not to just stay here until we know something more definite," Kelli insisted.

"But you're too young to be left—" he sputtered.

"Oh, here we go again." Kelli threw her hands into the air and began pacing back and forth in front of his desk. "Think how disruptive it will be for the children."

"I don't know—" he said, a scowl wrinkling his brow.

"Look, let's at least give it a try. It would be a lot easier on me and the children if we could stay here in familiar territory."

He had to admit what she said made sense. Reluctantly, he agreed. "Is there anything you need? I'll be back Tuesday night. Oh, I just don't know." Peter's voice drifted off into a sigh.

In an effort to ease his concern, she rested her hand on his. "We'll be fine here, don't worry. We have plenty of food, medicine, wood, and heating oil. What else do we need? And Roger's within calling distance, thanks to this baby." She patted the black metal box. "We'll do just fine."

"Be careful, OK?" he asked, running the back of his rough hand tenderly along her jaw line.

At the sound of footsteps, they turned to see Pamela enter the library.

"Grandma says she's ready when you are. Lisa and I took her suitcases to the plane." Her disapproving glare surprised them both.

Peter scowled as he folded Kelli's hand into his. "I know the children will be fine with you. You care for them as you would your own. I'm still not comfortable thrusting such a large responsibility upon someone your age."

"My age! There you go again! I've never before met anyone so hung up on age. What are you, all of thirty-two or thirty-three? A real Methuselah, huh?" She stormed out. "I'm going to say goodbye to your mother," she called, slamming the door behind her.

The next two days dragged slowly by. Even the special activities she planned for the children didn't rush the hours.

Pamela developed a cough. Kelli worried when it settled deep in the little girl's chest. Noting Pamela's listlessness, Kelli moved Pamela into her own room for the night. She was surprised the child didn't object.

The girl lay quietly as Kelli read and prayed before getting into bed. Kelli had just settled down beneath her blankets when Pamela spoke, "Do you know that this is the first time you've done something special just for me?"

Tears clouded Kelli's eyes. She's right, Kelli realized. I've done special things with Lisa and spent lots of time cuddling Petey, but Pamela?

"Well, I'm glad you told me. We need to change that. I know, let's sneak downstairs for some hot cider."

Pamela readily agreed. Giggling in the stillness, the two tiptoed down to the kitchen. Pamela seemed wound up, wanting to talk. Her eyes darkened as she spoke of her grandmother's illness. Kelli remained silent, letting the child talk.

"When Mamma died, Daddy left for a while. He came up here to build this house. I kinda felt like I'd lost both my parents. But Grandma was always there whenever I needed her, even sometimes when I didn't. I think I'd die if I lost her too." The little girl stared into her empty mug.

"Pamela, we are praying for Grandma, placing her in Jesus' hands. Right now, our job is to trust Him with her life. He knows how important she is to you. And He'll do what's best, just like He promised," Kelli said, patting the little girl's hand tenderly.

Suddenly, Pamela pulled her hand away from Kelli's. "You were comforting Daddy before he left, weren't you?" she questioned, her eyes narrowing slightly.

"Yes, sort of," Kelli said, uncertain of what might come next.

Pamela thought for a moment. "I'm glad," she admitted.

"Ready to sleep?" Kelli asked. The child nodded. Together they returned to Kelli's bedroom and settled down to sleep.

An hour before dawn, a faint whimper awakened Kelli. Switching on the light, she hurried to the child's side. "Oh, Honey, you're burning up. Let me take your temperature."

Kelli inserted the thermometer into Pamela's mouth. "Keep it under your tongue, Sweetheart. That's right." She waited, then removed it from the girl's mouth. "Oh, dear, it's 104°!" Recalling her mother's treatment for high fevers, Kelli drew the child's covers back and announced, "I think you need a little sponge bath, young lady."

"Now? In the middle of the night?" The child protested weakly.

"Now!" Kelli scooped the girl into her arms and rushed to the bathroom.

The tepid water and alcohol rub brought Pamela's temperature back into a safe range. Later, as Pamela dropped off to sleep, Kelli remembered the radio. Quietly, she tiptoed down the stairs to the library.

She flipped on the power switch. Picking up the hand-held microphone, she pressed the button on the side and called, "CQ, CQ, anyone on this frequency? This is KL7AOP looking for KL7BRR. This is KL7AOP looking for KL7BRR. Over."

Suddenly the radio came alive. "If you'd stop talking long enough for me to break in, I'd answer you," Roger teased, his voice heavy with sleep. "What's wrong? Over."

"If you'd be quiet, I'd tell you what's the matter," Kelli replied. "Pamela had a high fever tonight. It's down now, but I don't know for how long. She might have a touch of pneumonia. Does Suzanne keep any antibiotics on hand? Over."

"By the case KL7AOP. But she's not here; she's with a patient. I'll check in with her and get back to you. Don't worry, ya' hear? Over."

"I'll be listening for your transmission. Over." Kelli sighed and leaned back against the chair.

She'd almost fallen asleep when she remembered Pamela. She ran upstairs to check on the sleeping child. She touched Pamela's forehead. "Cool!" she whispered, "Thank You, Lord."

Returning to the library, she sank into the leather armchair to await Roger's call. Exhausted, Kelli fought sleep, but soon lost the battle.

Awaking with a start, Kelli panicked. "Oh no! What time is it?" She ran up the stairs to Pamela's bedside again. As she bent to feel the child's forehead, a voice startled her.

"Her temperature is normal." Suzanne stepped out of the shadows, looking every bit like the doctor she was.

Kelli whirled about and gasped, "Where'd you come from? Oh, I'm so glad you're here."

"Roger insisted. He's down in the kitchen trying to scramble up a breakfast. You look like you could use one. Go on now, doctor's orders. I'll take over here."

Obediently, Kelli made her way to the kitchen, where Roger had made himself at home with a big bowl of cereal and milk.

"Thanks so much for coming," she said, "I can't tell you how relieved I was to see your sister. You're a great friend." Kelli reached across the table and patted Roger's arm.

With his mouth full of Cheerios, Roger grinned up at Kelli and nodded but kept on chewing. She turned to remove a bowl from the cupboard when she heard a familiar voice behind her.

"What's happening? What are you doing here at this hour?" Peter demanded, glaring down at the startled Roger.

"Oh, Peter, I'm so glad you're back," Kelli interrupted. "Pamela had a fever of 104°. Suzanne is upstairs with her now."

His flash of irritation turned to distress as he realized his error. Without a word, Peter turned and dashed up the stairs to his child's bedside.

Roger's smile fell as he saw Kelli watching the departing Peter. "I wish your face lighted up for me like that when I enter the room," he drawled.

"Tsk! Roger, stop teasing. Have another bowl of cereal. I'll be right back," she called as she hurried from the room.

Chapter 8
Facing the Facts

Kelli ran the feather duster across the book-lined shelves and turned to dust Peter's desk when her eye caught sight of the desk calendar. It had been more than a month since Grandma had moved to Anchorage, and from all reports, her condition hadn't improved. Test after test had been taken, yet the doctors seemed to be no closer to a diagnosis.

Divided between his work and the hospital, Peter dropped in at the cabin for short visits. Always, he arranged to be gone before nightfall. The children grew to depend on Kelli more and more, though her practiced eye noted the sadness each of them harbored.

With Peter preoccupied over his mother, the weekly radio visits stopped, forcing Kelli to write to her parents each week.

"You know, Mom," she wrote, "letting go of Jeff was difficult, but I'm afraid that when I leave these kids, it will be much worse. You know, I'm not one to do anything halfway, including this thing called 'love.'" She didn't mention that her growing fondness didn't stop with Lisa, Petey, and Pamela, because she still refused to admit to herself just how much she'd come to care for their father.

With Christmas only two months away, Kelli encouraged the children to plan their Christmas gifts. For hours, they poured over a shopping catalog until Kelli was sure she could recite the description of every sale item in the entire book. After counting their individual hoards of cash, the children filled out an order blank.

"I'll place the envelope here on the table, so when your father comes home he'll be sure to mail it when he goes," she explained. "That way it will have a head start over waiting for Mr. Lee's supply run." The three children solemnly agreed.

"May we stay up until Daddy gets home?" Pamela pleaded. "He's been gone for so long."

"Yeah, I'd like to know how Grandma's doing," Lisa urged.

50

"Please, Miss Kelli, please?" Petey chimed in, looking pitifully into her face. Kelli frowned, scowled, then shook her finger at each of the children.

"On one condition. All baths must be taken and everyone must be in their pj's, ready for bed. Maybe we can take turns telling stories around the fire."

All three children danced about, squealing with delight.

"And we can toast marshmallows?" Lisa suggested, her blond pigtails bouncing unevenly.

"And roast hot dogs?" Petey added.

"Sure, why not? I'll get the food; you take your baths. Scoot now!" She dashed to the kitchen as the children raced up the stairs.

Later, Kelli and the children snuggled down before the fire. All the favorite tales of ferocious bears, rampaging mountain lions, and stalking wolves were repeated. The children screamed with laughter as Kelli told about some of the silly adventures she and Rhonda, her big sister, had.

The clock in the library gonged eleven times.

"Oh dear, I didn't realize it was so late. Your father probably stopped at the Lee's for the night. He'll be here when you awaken in the morning," Kelli coaxed.

"But you promised." Petey's lower lip protruded into a definite pout.

"Well, I guess, but if he isn't home in one hour, we'll all go to bed, OK?" They readily agreed.

Wrapped in soft, warm quilts, the twins cuddled up on the floor in front of the hearth, while Petey curled up in Kelli's lap.

"Once upon a time there was a handsome young prince. His name was Jonathan. Jonathan was a very special prince because he was being trained to become king of his country," Kelli began. "Would you like to be a prince or perhaps a princess?" She leaned forward, only to discover that her audience had fallen asleep. Petey snuggled closer, causing her to put her arm more securely around the child.

"Oh well, so much for Jonathan," she thought. "I'll just lean back and rest my eyes for a few minutes, then carry them to their bedrooms."

Before many seconds passed, Kelli drifted into the mystical kingdom between consciousness and sleep. Familiar faces floated past—family members, childhood friends, Petey, Lisa, Pamela, Grandma, and, as always, Peter. A creaking sound awakened her.

Her eyes popped open in surprise. "Peter? Peter!"

"S-s-s-h," he whispered, his face disturbingly close. "I didn't mean to wake you," he breathed, lifting the sleeping child from her arms.

"Oh, I'm sorry. I fell asleep, I guess," she admitted, blushing uncomfortably under his gaze. Kelli struggled to get out of the rocker.

"Relax, I've already carried the twins upstairs. I'll deposit Petey in his bed and be right back down. Don't run away," he added.

Knowing he was probably hungry, Kelli flew about the kitchen, heating the leftover stew. She placed three of his favorite sourdough biscuits in the microwave oven to warm, listening for his return.

When Peter entered the kitchen, Kelli hastened to apologize, "I'm sorry the children were up so late, but they've been pretty lonely for you. And when they begged to stay up until you arrived, I felt sorry for them and—"

"Hey, it's fine," he assured her. "I trust your judgment. You should know that by now. M-m-m! This lentil stew is fantastic. I guess you're more than half a cook after all," he teased, biting into one of the reheated biscuits she'd placed before him. "Aren't you having any?"

"I'd better go to bed. The kids will be waking early and I—" She edged away from the table.

His eyes reflected the same sad-eyed-turtle look Petey had when the young boy was feeling mistreated. "I hate eating alone. At least have a cup of hot chocolate with me, like old times. I've missed that, you know, having to be gone so often."

Feeling somewhat trapped, she sat down in the chair across the table from him. "No, I didn't know that," she whispered nervously.

For a while he studied her without speaking; then he broke the silence. "I've really appreciated your help these last few months. I couldn't have handled everything without you." His eyes searched hers for hint of response. "You're the best thing that's happened to this family in a long time."

"Well, that's good to hear. And how is your mother?" Kelli asked, attempting to change the subject.

"Not so good. The doctors haven't discovered the cause for her headaches yet. She still wants to fly to Boston after Christmas. Suzanne agrees with her. If the weather holds, we'll all spend the holidays with her in Anchorage. Suzanne and Roger will celebrate with us."

"Great! The children will love seeing her again," Kelli admitted.

Peter tipped his soup bowl in order to get the last spoonful. "I hope it's something you'll enjoy too. After all, you've been cooped up here for some time now, and unfairly, I might add."

Noting Peter's empty bowl, she reached for the pot of stew. "Here, there's lots more." She emptied the last of the stew into Peter's bowl. "Christmas in Anchorage sounds great to me."

"Thank you. I shouldn't eat any more, as late as it is. But this is good stuff! Anyway, last week Suzanne went to a medical seminar in Seattle and stopped in to see Mother on her way back. She's been a real encouragement," he admitted.

"I'm glad she was there to help. Friends like Roger and Suzanne are hard to come by," Kelli admitted, surprised by the sudden scowl she saw on Peter's face.

"Look," she began, "you must be pretty tired. I know I am. It's already 2:00 a.m. We can talk in the morning." Kelli scooted her chair away from the table and stood to leave.

"You're right. Go on up to sleep. But I won't be here in the morning. I promised Suzanne that I'd pick her up around nine or ten. I might as well head down to the trading post and catch a few winks there." Peter yawned and leaned back in his chair.

"Oh," Kelli said, her voice filled with regret, "the children were so looking forward to spending some time with you."

Peter glanced into Kelli's bewildered eyes. "Well, maybe I can run upstairs and give them each a kiss and hug before I leave."

Kelli shook her head in disbelief. "Excuse me for overstepping my position, but your children need more than a quick kiss and hug from you. I don't understand why you can't go into your quarters for the rest of the night; then in the morning you'd at least have a few hours with them before you had to leave again." She attempted to hide her disappointment.

"Kelli," he began, then paused. "There is nothing I would rather do than just that. Surely you understand why I can't."

"No." Kelli shook her head, more distraught than ever.

"It wouldn't be right to jeopardize your reputation by staying here in the house alone with you."

"But this is your home," she argued.

"You really don't understand what I'm saying, do you?" he said, his eyes darkening.

"I'm sorry—" she stammered. Her hands flew up to hide her reddening face. "I don't want to come between you and your children. Perhaps I should cut my term of employment short under the circumstances. I never dreamed—It never crossed my mind that that might be the reason—"

"Which goes to show just how young you really are." Peter stepped up behind her and laid his hand on her shoulder. "Kelli, please don't turn away from me. I treasure you and what you're doing for my children too much to risk allowing vain regrets to enter our friendship. I wouldn't hurt you for anything; please know that," Peter assured her. "And if it will make you feel better, I'll postpone tomorrow's trip, come back, and spend the entire day with the kids. Will that make you happier?"

Kelli bit her lip. What could she say? How could she answer? Finally she replied, "Maybe you'd better locate another tutor or arrange for them to stay with relatives in the lower forty-eight."

"And tear them apart even more? They love you. You're the only source of stability they have now that my mom's gone. What would it accomplish if you left now? Don't you see, I still would have to finish my government contract here, so I wouldn't be with them in California. And another woman? No way. Having you around has been quite enough, thank you," he argued.

Kelli gasped and stiffened. "I'm sorry I've been so difficult—" she started.

"*Difficult* isn't the right word," he said, taking a deep breath.

His words cut Kelli deeply, pushing all his earlier compliments from her mind. She knew her eyes registered her pain, but she possessed no guile with which to hide her feelings.

"Don't look at me like that, Kelli. I only meant—"

Her lower lip quivered as she interrupted, "I know what you meant."

"No, you don't." He ran one hand through his hair in frustration.

Again Kelli blushed uncomfortably. "I think I do."

"When I saw Petey asleep in your arms, I wanted to—I'm sorry. I have no right. I know how much you hate to have me mention your age, but like it or not, you are just beginning to live. You're fresh and alive, and innocent," he added, pounding his fist on the kitchen counter, "and I'm a married man. Or at least, in my mind I am, and probably always will be."

Kelli watched wordlessly as Peter paced the length of the kitchen, then back again. "I have no right to take advantage of your isolation from young men your own age to ease my loneliness. If we'd met ten years ago—" His voice drifted off into a raspy whisper.

"I'd be twelve years old," she whispered, then blushed.

"See? Twelve years old," he groaned, shaking his head in defeat. "I'm sorry. I'll be back in time for breakfast."

Chapter 9
Grizzly!

Kelli watched winter trickle down the hillsides, across the lake, to the river valley like French icing on a chocolate cake. She noted how the harsh frosts lingered longer each morning after the sun appeared in the sky.

One morning she found the valley submerged in a deep, white silence. The vibrant-blue lake and matching sky, the evergreens of the forest, and the newly fallen snow made her wish she could capture this magical world on canvas.

The children squealed with delight when they discovered what to them was a fairyland, created especially for their pleasure. Kelli decided to make the day not only fun filled, but also a learning experience.

After breakfast chores were completed, she instructed them on how to identify animal tracks in the snow. Lisa was the first to locate a specimen. "Look, rabbit tracks, Miss Kelli," Lisa squealed excitedly. Kelli examined the discovery. "You're right. They're definitely rabbit tracks."

"Miss Kelli, over here!" Pamela cried, "Aren't these deer tracks?" Kelli inspected Pamela's latest find. She traced the print with her gloved finger. "They're a little big for the white-tailed deer—could be a caribou or moose." Pamela shivered with excitement at Kelli's pronouncement.

"T'ain't fair!" sniffed Petey, "I can't find any."

"*Isn't* Petey. It *isn't* fair," Kelli reminded. She rezipped his parka and rustled in her pockets for a tissue for his runny nose. "And be patient. Your turn will come."

"Let's make angels." Lisa plopped down in a spot of unbroken snow and began waving her arms frantically.

"Humph! Girl's stuff," Petey muttered, stomping back toward the cabin.

"Don't stray far, Petey. It's almost time to make the sweetbread for Thanksgiving," Kelli warned, as she joined Lisa in making angels.

Pamela stood over her snow imprint admiring her work. "You know, my mamma used to tell stories about the snow angels she used to make where she grew up in Massachusetts. They have lots of snow there too."

Kelli sat up and brushed the snow from her shoulders and back. "Yeah, lots of snow. I'll bet she made some beauties."

"Prob'ly so," the girl whispered.

Kelli jumped to her feet, grabbed a handful of snow, and began forming a snowball. "How about making a snowman or two?" she asked. "I'll make the base. Who wants to make the head?"

Pamela and Lisa immediately began rolling the snow for the rest of their snowman. After Pamela poked the last pebble in place for the snowman's eyes, Lisa suggest they make an entire family—their family. After finishing the last snowman, they trudged back to the house to get warm.

"Don't track the snow onto the carpet. Brush each other off before you go inside," Kelli gasped, running to keep up with the two girls.

As she entered the house, Kelli called, "Petey? Petey! We're back. It's time to shape the bread into loaves. Petey? I'll bet the little stinker fell asleep," she decided, running upstairs to his room.

"Petey?" His bed stood empty. "Girls," she stuck her head out into the hall, "check to see if Petey is in the library or in your dad's room. He's not up here anywhere. He couldn't have gone far, could he?"

Kelli searched the house thoroughly. Since they knew all the best hiding places, the girls conducted their own search.

"I'm scared," Lisa sniffed when she returned to the living room. "He's not anywhere."

"Stop it, Lisa," Kelli scolded. "He has to be somewhere. Did you see him go toward the woods or perhaps the lake?" Kelli gasped at the terrible thought. "What if he's fallen through the ice?"

"No, I saw him come back here," Pamela insisted.

"Could he have gotten to the lake by any other route?" Kelli's fingers refused to cooperate as she rezipped her parka and wrapped her woolen scarf around her neck.

"Not in this deep snow. The only paths cleared are the one to the lake and the one to the airstrip," Pamela reminded.

"The airstrip! Listen carefully. Pamela, you and Lisa stick together. Take the path to the lake. Look for his tracks in the snow. If you spot them, yell. I'll hear you. In the meantime, I'll head to the airstrip. Remember, stay together." Kelli started out the back door.

"I can't. I just can't!" Lisa wailed. "What if there are bears or wolves or something out there?"

"Bears are hibernating by now. And we would have heard wolves if they were still in the area," Kelli reminded. At least I hope so, she thought. "OK, we'll meet back here in ten minutes. Got it?"

"Right!" The two girls trudged through the snow toward the lake. Kelli ran, slipped, and slid down the other path toward the cleared airstrip. The snow near the house was too disturbed from their earlier play to identify any tracks that might be Petey's.

"Petey! Petey!" Kelli called, first on one side of the path, then the other. She was so busy scanning the woods that she tripped over a large stick. Picking herself up, she identified it as Petey's favorite walking stick. She recognized it by the point Petey had whittled on one end.

But it was what imprinted the snow next to the stick that turned Kelli's knees to tapioca pudding. Bear tracks! Stifling the urge to run for the cabin, she followed the tracks of the animal and the young boy.

"Breathe deeply. Stay calm," she ordered herself. "Because the prints are near each other doesn't necessarily mean Petey found the bear. The beast could be miles from here by now."

The cold wind whipped across her cheeks as she reached the strip. Tears stung her face, though she was hardly aware she was crying.

"Father, please watch over Petey wherever he is," she begged. "Help me to find him before anything happens to him."

A sudden movement by the left side of the storage shed caught Kelli's attention. Spotting Petey's red jacket, she ran toward where he stood.

"You little scamp. Now is not the time to play hide 'n seek! You really had us—" Kelli's words froze midsentence. Her eyes widened in terror. Less than twenty feet beyond where Petey crouched, stood the epitome of her wildest nightmare—a giant grizzly bear.

Standing on his hind legs, with his back to Kelli, the bear appeared to be trying to decide what to do about Petey. Fortunately Kelli was upwind from the bear, and the animal hadn't picked up her scent.

"Oh Lord," she prayed, "it's worse than I imagined. What shall

I do? Help me!" A noise behind her caused her to glance over her shoulder. The two girls were standing at the edge of the woods. Frantically, she waved them back.

An idea began to develop, and she prayed again. "Father, give me the strength I need to do what I have to do. Make it work, if it's Your will." Taking a deep breath, Kelli made her way toward the bear, still clutching Petey's sharp walking stick in her gloved hand. She circled the shed, careful to stay out of Petey's view lest he see her and give her away.

As she stepped around the shed into Petey's line of vision, she drew back the stick and jabbed it into the bear's backside and screamed at the same time, "Run, Petey! Run home to Pamela!"

The bear yelped in surprise and whirled about to identify his attacker. When the bear spotted Kelli, he bounded toward her.

Stumbling over her own feet, Kelli disappeared around the corner of the storage shed in the opposite direction from Petey. Her lungs ached from the sudden influx of cold arctic air. She fell through the open door of the storage shed. She slammed the heavy door closed and dropped the crossbar into place.

The bear lunged at the door again and again. Ominous creaks and groans warned her that the door wasn't designed to withstand such an assault.

"Father, help the kids get to the house safely. Help Pamela to have enough sense to radio for help," Kelli wailed, while shoving heavy cartons against the vibrating door. After every available box stood between her and the locked door, Kelli stopped long enough to wipe the sweat from her face. "And I thought it was cold outside?" she quipped.

Minutes dragged by. Kelli's arms ached from lifting the boxes while the bear's attacks became less forceful and less frequent. In spite of her fears, the dark interior of the shed wrapped Kelli in a cocoon of security. Whether she slept or not, she didn't know. But, suddenly, panic returned. The attack on the door began again.

"Kelli! Kelli! Are you all right? Kelli, for pity sake, open this door!" The voice demanded.

It was Peter. "Oh, Peter, th-th-the bear? Is he gone?" she stuttered.

Peter laughed. "Do you think I would be standing here if he weren't?" he asked.

Kelli struggled to shove the shipping crates out of the way. Finally, the doorway was cleared, and she lifted the bar. Peter rushed in and swept her into his arms.

"Oh, Kelli, are you all right? I never should have left you out here alone. You fool! How could you attack a full-grown bear? What a stupid thing to do! Oh, but I love you for it." His words tumbled over one another. He held her so tightly she began to think she would have fared better with a hug from the bear.

"I'm OK. I'm OK. But is Petey safe? Are the girls all right? Where's the bear?" Kelli sputtered, trying to learn everything at once.

"The kids are fine. Are you sure you're not hurt?" He pushed her damp curls from her forehead as if checking for injuries.

Kelli pushed his hands away from her face. "I'm all right, but how did you get here so soon?" she asked, pushing against his suede parka, to put some space between them.

"I had just landed at the trading post to drop off Suzanne when Pamela radioed for help. I'm lucky Roger had already fueled up or I'd have forgotten." Reluctantly, he released his hold on Kelli. "She told Roger that you were trapped in the shed by a bear and that you actually stabbed the bear with a stick," he reported incredulously.

"Yes, go on," Kelli urged.

"Why, I left immediately, of course. Suzanne almost had to tie Roger to the cash register to keep him from coming with me. He sure thinks a lot of you," Peter added, eyeing her suspiciously.

"And then what?" she replied, meeting his glare straight on.

"When I landed, the roar of the engines frightened the bear. I saw him high-tailing it into the woods at the far end of the field." Peter's description of the bear's retreat caused Kelli to laugh in spite of her inability to stop shaking.

"I've never been so scared in my life," she admitted. "I know it was risky to stab the bear, but I couldn't think of any other way to get his attention off Petey." Kelli's knees seemed to be melting beneath her. She staggered and grinned sheepishly as Peter reached to catch her.

"We have three very frightened children back at the house. Do you feel up to walking, or should I carry you?" Peter questioned, searching her face for clues to her real condition.

"I'm sure I can make it," she insisted, pulling away from Peter's arms.

The deepening twilight of the Alaskan afternoon surrounded them. The snow crunched beneath Peter's boots as he wrapped his arm about her shoulders and drew her close. "You're one in a million, Girl." His breath warmed the side of her face. "I don't know what we did to deserve you."

Three minutes later they entered the brightly-lighted kitchen, where the three children stood wide-eyed with fear. Peter fielded all their questions as he led Kelli out to the living room sofa. "She's OK, just a little weak." Pamela and Lisa threw themselves into her arms.

"While we waited for Daddy, Pamela insisted we finish making the bread. I hope we did it right," Lisa asked, her face stained with tears. "We turned the heat down under the stew so it wouldn't burn too."

"You sweetheart," Kelli sniffed, turning to Pamela. "You think of everything."

"I-I-I'm sorry!" Petey's big brown eyes filled to overflowing as he walked slowly toward Kelli. "It was my fault," he whimpered.

"Honey," Kelli drew him into her lap, "don't blame yourself. The important thing is that we're all safe."

"Miss Kelli, do ya know what? When I saw the bear, I prayed. That's why I was standing so still; I was praying," the boy admitted.

"Me too," Lisa added, her eyes solemn and round. "I almost screamed when I saw Miss Kelli jab that bear. I think God kept me from screaming, don't you?" Kelli nodded in agreement.

"When Petey began to run toward the woods, Pamela ran to him and dragged him all the way to the cabin," Lisa explained.

"She ripped my jacket too."

"Don't worry," Kelli said, "I'll fix it tomorrow. That was very brave of you, Pamela. I was afraid the bear might chase Petey instead of me."

"You know, Kids, you and Miss Kelli are turning my ideas about God upside down," Peter confessed, lifting his son from Kelli's lap into his own arms. "We have lots to be thankful for this Thanksgiving Day," Peter admitted.

At the supper table, the children each retold his part in the great adventure until, before long, all were laughing hysterically as they recounted the picture of Kelli poking the bear with the stick.

Peter glanced at the clock. "I think you'd better get a good night's sleep tonight. I need to fly down to the trading post tonight, but I'll be back in the morning, and I expect you all to be ready to leave," he reminded. "In the meantime, I'll straighten the kitchen while you children take your baths and get to bed. I'll be up to tuck you in after a bit."

"We haven't had family worship yet," Petey reminded.

Peter stood and lifted his son from the chair. "Miss Kelli is pretty tired tonight. It's been an eventful day. So maybe we can just recite a verse and have prayer?" The children gathered about him, pulling Kelli into the tight family circle. Together they recited Kelli's favorite text; then Pamela prayed.

When the children disappeared upstairs, Kelli began collecting the dishes from the table. Peter came up behind her and removed the dishes from her hands.

"I'll take care of everything. You toddle up to bed," he said, guiding her through the living room, to the foot of the stairs. "I'll be back to pick you up around eight or so, if that's all right." Then cupping her hands in his, he gently kissed her fingertips. "Sweet dreams now, ya' hear?"

As she stumbled up the stairs to her room, Kelli realized her memories of her Alaskan interlude would stay with her much longer than she'd ever imagined.

Chapter 10
Silver Skates

Thanksgiving vacation with its whirlwind of shopping and sightseeing passed too quickly for Kelli. With Grandma leaving for the East immediately after Christmas, Kelli realized that her goodbye after Christmas would be final to their friendship.

"Why go back to the cabin?" Grandma asked, "It's such a short time between holidays, and I get so lonely here by myself. What do you think, Peter?"

"Would the children be too much for you?" Peter questioned.

"Not with Kelli here," Grandma said to the children's delight.

"I have to go back. However, I'm sure that I could manage alone for a few weeks," he admitted.

"Nonsense!" Suzanne interrupted. "Close up the cabin and stay with us."

"I'd like it better if Kelli were coming back too," Roger teased.

Kelli noticed that everyone except Peter laughed.

"I could spend the rest of this week in Anchorage to analyze some related data," Peter casually announced.

"Well, I have to get back. I told my relief doctor I'd be back Monday," Suzanne sighed.

"And I have inventory staring me in the face if I plan to take time off at Christmas," Roger growled, wrinkling his nose with distaste.

"Then it's settled," Grandma said, clapping her hands triumphantly. "I'll get to enjoy my little bunnies a while longer."

Roger and Suzanne flew out of Anchorage the next morning. As the rest of them returned to the rented Jeep, Grandma whispered something to the children and made an announcement.

"The children and I have some very important shopping to do. Peter, unless your research is urgent, you could show Kelli more of the city sights, and the children and I will see you back at the apartment tonight."

"Are you sure you feel strong enough to wrestle with the children in this Christmas rush?" Kelli queried anxiously.

"We've already discussed it. My medicine seems to be working well, so I'll do just fine. Now, if you'll just drop us off downtown, we'll take a taxi home," Grandma insisted.

Peter grinned and glanced at Kelli. "It's a waste of energy arguing with Mother. She'll win in the end, anyway," he chuckled.

After leaving Grandma and the children off in front of the large department store, Peter eased the Jeep into the midmorning traffic.

"Do you ice-skate?" Peter asked, without taking his eyes off the traffic.

"Oh yes. When Rhonda and I were kids my folks would take us to Lloyd's Center. It's a large shopping plaza with an open-air skating rink right in the middle of it." Kelli's face glowed with the memory. "We skated while our parents shopped!"

Peter turned toward Kelli and said, "Believe it or not, I learned to ice-skate in southern California. Having been raised in Massachusetts, Liz loved ice-skating. She insisted I learn too." He paused, then added, "So you want to give it a whirl?"

Kelli looked down at her treasured Pendleton wool plaid skirt and grimaced. "I'll need to change clothes first."

"Me too. Nothing short of denim survives the spills I take," Peter joked, turning off the main thoroughfare into the street leading to his mother's apartment.

After a quick change of clothes and a pickles-and-cheese sandwich each, they were off to the rink.

Kelli had forgotten how much fun gliding across the ice could be. Except for an elderly couple skating together, Kelli and Peter had the rink to themselves.

"C'mon, Slow-poke," Peter challenged, "I'll race you to the wall."

"OK, you're on!" Kelli dug her blades into the ice and took off.

"Hey, no fair!" Peter shouted, in hot pursuit, "I didn't say Go."

Kelli laughed as she touched the end-zone railing. "I did, though. Too bad."

"Oh, you want to play that way. OK," he tapped her shoulder and skated away, "you're it for tag."

"No, you don't!" Kelli squealed, swerving to follow his zigzag pattern down the ice.

Skating at full speed, Peter glanced over his shoulder to determine how close Kelli might be and missed seeing a ripple in the surface of the ice. Momentarily thrown off balance, Peter fought to right himself.

His weird contortions, with arms and legs flailing, made Kelli double over with laughter, causing her to miss seeing the same ripple. Her final landing proved to be softer than his. She fell, face down, sprawled across his flattened back.

"I'll never walk again," he moaned, as she rolled onto the ice. "For such a wisp of a woman, you sure pack a wallop!"

Peter climbed to his feet. "Here, let me help," he said, helping her to her feet. Slipping his arm around her waist, Peter took her other hand in his free one. They glided across the ice to the strains of piped-in Christmas carols until the management announced that the rink would close in ten minutes.

Peter knelt before Kelli. His fingers moved nimbly, untying the skates' lacings. "In the mood for pizza?" he asked.

"Sounds yummy!" Kelli imagined the familiar aroma of heating sauce.

At the pizza parlor, Peter led her to a secluded booth and slid in opposite her. Once the teenage waiter took their order, Peter gazed unashamedly across the table at Kelli. He reached across and took her hands in his. Turning them over, he traced her lifelines on her palms.

"I haven't had so much fun in years," he said, his voice husky with emotion. "I didn't admit it when you first arrived, but if you hadn't come to help with the children this year, I would possibly have had to forgo my research and return to California."

"You're always complimenting me. I'm sure you would have found someone else," Kelli whispered, staring helplessly at their hands in the center of the table. Alternately, she wished he'd release them, then prayed he'd never let go.

"Gratitude, that's all he feels," she warned herself. "That's the way it is, and that's the way it's going to stay."

Kelli withdrew her hands from his, saying, "I think I'll visit the ladies' room before the food arrives. My hands feel grimy from falling on the ice." She stood and walked from the room.

"You've fallen in love. There's no doubt about it," Kelli scolded herself. You've lost your heart to a man who belongs to a dead woman." When she returned to the booth, Kelli observed that during her absence, Peter's mood had lightened. For the rest of the day, it remained so between them.

Peter changed his plans to return to the cabin and during the days to come, Christmas shopping with mysterious packages stuffed in every closet, giggles, and constant whispering kept the children occupied.

On Christmas Eve, Roger arrived, weighted down with gaily-wrapped boxes of all shapes and sizes. Kelli told the Christmas story to the children, and, after tucking them all in for the night, she headed for the kitchen. "I'll finish the sugar cookies, Gram, if you'll head for bed," Kelli urged. Grandma didn't demur.

She had just placed the last sheet of sugar cookies into the oven when Roger came out to join her.

"May I help? I haven't decorated cookies since I was a kid." Roger picked up a frosted star cookie and sprinkled it with red crystals.

Kelli nodded and pointed to the supplies. "Help yourself."

Sitting across the table from one another, Kelli and Roger brushed the frostings on the cookies. When the last Santa had been "dressed" and stacked in a plastic container, she turned to find Roger staring at her.

"Roger? Are you all right?" she inquired, waving her hand before his eyes.

"You're gone on Peter, aren't you?" he asked.

Kelli choked and sputtered. "I—ah—well, what kind of question is that?"

"I can see it in your eyes whenever he's around," he said, smiling sadly. "I tried to warn you, ya know, about Liz, I mean."

Kelli stared at the ceiling for a second, then answered, "I know. You're a good friend, Roger." She turned to the sink and washed the frosting off her fingers.

When she turned to face him, she closed her eyes and rubbed her forehead as if in pain. "Please, don't say anything to anyone, especially Peter."

Roger didn't have time to answer before Peter and Suzanne burst through the front door, laughing and shaking snow from their ski jackets.

"Hi, you two! Those cookies smell scrumptious. Is there anything hot to drink?" Suzanne asked, hurrying to the stove. Peter remained standing in the doorway, looking as if he'd been punched in the stomach.

"I'll hang up the coats," he muttered and left the kitchen.

"What was that all about?" Suzanne questioned, looking from her brother to Kelli, then back again.

"What was what all about?" Kelli paled slightly and inched her way toward the kitchen door. "If anyone is hungry, there's homemade mushroom soup in the refrigerator. If you all will excuse me, I think I'll just head off to bed."

"No problem," Suzanne called. "I wonder what came over Peter?"

Chapter 11
Christmas Holidays

Kelli couldn't sleep that night. By the time she finally did drift off, three starry-eyed bodies bounded into her room and pounced on the bed.

"Wake up, Miss Kelli!" Lisa said, shaking Kelli's arm. "You and Dr. Lee are lazybones this morning. Everyone else is ready to open presents."

"I'll be ready in five minutes," Kelli groaned. "But you'll have to wake up Dr. Lee," she said, pointing to the hide-a-bed by the window.

"I'm awake! I'm awake! Promise!" Suzanne squealed as they bounded toward her.

"Don't bother getting dressed. No one else is," Petey advised as he scooted out of the room.

Horrified, Pamela rushed to clarify. "He means we're all still in our pj's and robes."

Suzanne laughed. "I think we get the idea, Pamela," she answered.

Kelli yawned, slipped on her robe, and ran a brush through her hair. "Here goes," she thought. " 'Tis the season to be jolly."

Yawning, Suzanne followed Kelli into the living room. The three children had already circled the tree like a war party attacking a wagon train.

Petey located one particular package and thrust it in Kelli's lap. "Open mine first, Miss Kelli," he begged.

"Hmm! I wonder what this can be," Kelli murmured, squeezing the soft, bulky package. "It feels cuddly." His eyes glistened as the wrapper quickly fell to her lap. "A stuffed animal—a grizzly bear, in fact! How appropriate!" Kelli exclaimed, kissing the little boy's cheek.

Other gifts followed until all the packages from under the tree had been opened. While everyone was occupied with his own gifts,

Peter moved to the side of Kelli's chair and dropped a small box into her lap. "I have something for you, too, if you want it," he said. Before she could react, he left the room.

Kelli looked about, hoping no one noticed her shaking hands as she unwrapped the tiny box. Upon lifting the lid, Kelli caught her breath. Centered on deep blue velvet lay an intricately-detailed silver pin in the shape of ice skates. "Oh," she whispered breathlessly.

"What is it, Miss Kelli?" Lisa peeked into Kelli's hands. "Did Daddy give that to you?"

"It's beautiful. Peter? Where did he go?" she asked. She found him in the kitchen standing by the sink.

"Peter?" Kelli shyly entered the kitchen. "I'm overwhelmed," she said. "I hardly know what to say. It's exquisite," Kelli whispered. "Why did you think I might not want it?"

"Well, after last night—" He walked to the sink, filled a glass with water, and gulped it down.

"What about last night?" she insisted. "I don't understand."

"It's none of my business—you and Roger. You're young. You're free. So's he. I don't know why I didn't think of it sooner. You'd be a good match for him, settle him down a bit. If you'll excuse me, I'll get back to the children," Peter muttered, as he brushed past her to leave the room.

"Peter," she breathed, knowing he couldn't hear her, "you've got it all wrong."

In the months following, Peter came and went from the cabin at irregular intervals. Whenever he did return for a day, he made a point of devoting all of his time to Kelli and the children. He took them snowmobiling, ice fishing, tobogganing and cross-country skiing. Though Kelli didn't enjoy fishing, she loved speeding across the frozen lake on the snowmobile.

Wednesday's mail was the highlight of Kelli's week. Grandma's letters from Boston were upbeat and positive. Kelli's parents' letters were filled with the anticipation of having her home again.

Kelli tried to have hot soup and homemade bread ready for Roger when he made his weekly grocery drop. Same old Roger, she thought. Just as friendly as ever. What is it that makes me think of Roger as a friend and Peter as—a what?

One Wednesday, after Roger had left a new supply of groceries and Kelli was preparing spaghetti for supper, Lisa burst into the kitchen. "There's a gigantic storm blowing in off the Bering Sea tonight. The 'hams' are all talking about it on the radio."

Kelli continued chopping the garlic cloves to put in the skillet. "Hmm, that's nice, Honey."

"I wish Daddy were here. I hate it when a bad storm comes and we're all alone," Lisa confessed.

"I know, but we're not alone, remember?" Kelli sprinkled sweet basil and oregano onto the garlic pieces browning in the fry pan. "How's Pamela feeling."

"She says her stomach hurts even worse than before." Lisa replied, sniffing the aromas from the browning garlic.

"Will you please watch this for a few moments while I check on her?" Kelli asked, as she rinsed her hands under the faucet. "Stir in the tomato sauce as soon as the garlic pieces are brown, OK?"

"Tsk! I know what to do," Lisa replied.

"Good, then do it," Kelli said hurrying from the room.

For days Pamela had complained about a stomachache. While it didn't seem to get any worse, it also didn't get any better. Kelli hurried up the stairs to the girls' room and tiptoed to Pamela's bedside. When she bent down and touched the child's forehead, she exclaimed, "You're burning with fever. Why didn't you tell me, Honey?"

Pamela's glassy eyes watered as she spoke, "I'm sorry. I didn't wanna complain. But my stomach hurts so bad. I threw up too."

"Pamela, you should have called me." Kelli picked up the thermometer off the night stand and stuck it in the girl's mouth.

"Are you sure it's your stomach? Let me feel your abdomen to be sure." Kelli tried to recall how the school nurse had tested her for appendicitis. "Tell me when it hurts," she said, gently probing below Pamela's rib cage and across her tummy.

"Eeiioowww!" Pamela screamed, spitting the thermometer across the bed.

"I'm sorry, Honey, but I had to be sure. I can't give you any aspirin for your temperature. It would hurt you more. I'll get a cool, wet washcloth to put on your head. Then I'm going to call Dr. Lee. She'll know what to do. Will you be all right for a few minutes?" Kelli asked.

Pamela nodded.

Kelli ran down the stairs two at a time. "I hope Suzanne's in. You poor kid," Kelli sighed. "You've surely had your share of sickness this winter. And if I'm right about this one, we're in trouble."

After describing Pamela's symptoms to Suzanne via the radio, Suzanne replied, "I hate to tell you this, but Roger hasn't returned yet from his grocery run. I don't expect him back until seven. To make things worse, I am afraid your diagnosis might be right. If Pamela's appendix is inflamed and it should burst—Over."

Kelli tried to speak, "But what should—" when she realized she'd forgotten to press the talk button. She tried again. "What can I do, Suzanne? Over."

"First, don't give her aspirin, and don't apply any heat. Somehow you've got to get her to me. I'd come to you, but I'm with a maternity patient about to deliver any minute. It's her first; she's having a difficult time. If only Roger were here! Over."

"Do you know where Peter is? Should I wait for Roger? Over." Kelli determinedly wiped the tears from her face.

"I have no answer for either question. Look, I'm going to sign off for now. My patient needs me desperately. Stay with Pamela and keep me posted. Have Lisa monitor the frequency. I'll call as soon as possible. I'm praying for you both, Kelli. Over."

For a moment, Kelli stared out the library window, considering her options. "I can't carry Pamela twenty miles over the mountains, leaving Petey and Lisa alone." Kelli tapped her fingers on the windowsill.

As she gazed out of the window, her eye caught sight of the gleaming yellow paint of the snowmobiles parked beneath protective tarps beside the front deck. "Hmm," she thought. "That machine could get us there. If I followed the frozen river, I wouldn't risk getting lost, and the snow wouldn't be as deep. Do I dare?" she wondered. "It might save Pamela's life." Kelli whirled about and ran to the foot of the stairs.

"Lisa, Petey! Come quickly. Hurry!" Wide-eyed, the frightened children ran to her side. "We're going for a snowmobile ride. Won't that be fun? We're going to take Pamela to the post, to Dr. Lee."

Chapter 12
Fighting the Blizzard

Lisa and Petey stared in frightened fascination as Kelli spat out orders like a marine sergeant. "Petey, round up all the sleeping bags and everyone's warmest parkas. Lisa, go make a batch of peanut-butter sandwiches and fill the thermos with hot cocoa. I'll call Dr. Lee and tell her my plan. If she thinks it's wise, we'll leave in fifteen minutes."

"There's a storm coming," Lisa reminded.

"Tonight, but not this afternoon. It's early," Kelli insisted. "I'll ride with Petey in my lap. And we'll pull you and Pamela on the toboggan like we did the day we went sledding on Bald Knob."

"I wanna ride on the toboggan too," Petey sniffed.

"We'll take turns, OK? Just do everything I ask. Both of you put on your insulated underwear, your warmest wool pants, two wool shirts, and your nylon ski suit," she ordered. "Ya got that?"

In record time, Kelli had filled the gas tank and radioed Suzanne of her plan. Suzanne reluctantly admitted that Pamela needed help as soon as possible. Kelli checked each child to be sure he was dressed warmly, then bundled herself.

Once the girls were safely on the toboggan and Petey was sitting securely in her lap, Kelli checked her watch again. Ten past two. At thirty miles per hour, taking into account the winding river, she figured they should reach the trading post by three-thirty or four at the latest.

She revved the noisy snowmobile engine, eased it carefully out of the yard and down to the west end of the lake that fed into the river running past the trading post.

For her personal worship that morning, Kelli had read 1 Peter 5:7. As the snowmobile bounced over the rough surface of the ice, the text kept repeating in her head. "Casting all your care upon him; for he careth for you."

"What a promise," she thought. "Out here in the wilderness,

racing against the sun and Pamela's infected appendix, it's up to You, Lord." Other texts came to mind. "I will never leave thee, nor forsake thee." Hebrews 13:5. "Lo, I am with you alway." Matthew 28:20. They tumbled through her memory as the racing machine bounced across ruts and ice mounds. "Take it easy," she reminded. "Think of Pamela."

Mile after mile, they traveled, hardly aware of passing time. Dark, ponderous clouds forced her to use the snowmobile's headlight. It took a few minutes before she was aware of the snowflakes pelting her exposed face. Remembering the uncomplaining boy on her lap, she stopped the snowmobile.

"Lisa, help Pamela put on her ski mask. You and Petey put yours on too," Kelli shouted above the whistling wind. "Would you mind holding Petey for a while, Lisa? I think I can fix it so that Pamela will still have enough room to stretch out."

After Petey snuggled into Lisa's lap, Kelli pulled a knitted mask over her face and twisted the hand controls. Sput . . . sput . . . sputter . . . sput! The snowmobile coughed, then stopped. Kelli climbed off and peered into the gas tank. "Hmm, plenty," she muttered, trying to start the machine again.

"I hate machines!" she bellowed at the top of her lungs, kicking the snowmobile with her boot. "Ouch!" Even through the thick snow boot, the blow registered. "Well, we can't stay here."

"Miss Kelli? If we unhitch the toboggan from the snowmobile, you and I could pull it the rest of the way," Lisa volunteered. "The trading post can't be too far from here."

Kelli climbed off the seat of the machine again. "If I figured it right, the post should be less than a mile away. OK! Let's at least try."

"What if I miscalculated the distance? What if the trading post is as much as ten miles or so further? What chance do we have of making it safely, with me walking and pulling three children on a toboggan? After all, Lisa will not be able to help pull the sled for very long. Talk about being a fool," she thought. "I really did it this time—risking not only my life, but theirs as well."

Trudging through the drifts of unbroken snow quickly exhausted Lisa until Kelli finally stopped. "Honey, get back on the sled and rest. I can handle it alone for a while," she said, her shoulders aching from the weight of the toboggan, her legs numb. Worse yet, it was getting darker by the minute.

Ominous night sounds echoed between the hills. "What's that?" Lisa whimpered, "It sounds like a lady crying. Maybe someone's been hurt."

Kelli listened to the spine-tingling wail. "I—I don't think so," she answered. "I think it's only a mountain lion. He's a long way away, don't you think?"

"Well it sounds like a woman to me," Lisa whined. "I'm scared."

"Come on, be brave. Petey and Pamela need your strength right now," Kelli encouraged, bending further into the weight of the toboggan. The blinding snowstorm made it difficult for Kelli to follow the meandering river.

Suddenly Lisa let out a scream. Kelli whirled about to see the child pointing ahead into the darkness. "Look, Miss Kelli, look! There's a light. I think it's a snowmobile light. It's Daddy. I just know it's Daddy!" Lisa screamed excitedly.

A groan from Pamela reminded them both that they still had a very sick patient on their hands.

"Sit still, Lisa. If it's your father, he'll be here in a minute," Kelli called over her shoulder as she tried to move the sled faster.

Within a few minutes, the one light divided into two. Kelli began laughing uncontrollably. "Thank You, Lord. Oh, thank You," she prayed as two snowmobiles roared up beside her.

"Oh, Daddy, you came for us. I knew you would," Lisa squealed, throwing herself into her father's arms. "Pamela has been so sick. We were really worried."

"And then the snowmobile broke down, and Miss Kelli had to pull the toboggan," Petey added, scrambling out of one of the sleeping bags.

While Lisa and Petey recited the tale of their adventure, Roger hitched up the toboggan to his snowmobile.

"Peter," Kelli reminded, "we still have an emergency situation here—Pamela's fever is high again even in this frigid weather."

"I've hitched the toboggan to my machine since it's more powerful than the one you're using, Peter," Roger said. "You kids get back in those sleeping bags now. We're heading for the trading post. Kelli, ride with Peter."

Without a word, Peter mounted the snowmobile. Kelli obediently hopped on behind him. Except for one or two disconcerting looks, he'd barely acknowledged Kelli's presence. She sensed the tension between them. Because of this sudden barrier, she tried to maintain her balance without touching him.

Over his shoulder Peter shouted, "Woman, will you hold on? I don't want to lose you on one of these corners. Lean against me for protection from the wind." She obeyed, too exhausted to cry and very thankful to be alive.

Chapter 13
Mrs. Karpenko—For a Moment

Peter stormed back and forth across Suzanne's office. "You reckless fool!" he shouted. "You and the children could have died out there! I was afraid we'd find you frozen to death in a snowbank."

"And your daughter could have died back at the cabin before help could arrive," Kelli reminded. "Suzanne agreed with me. There was nothing else I could do, don't you see? I had to try." Tears trickled down Kelli's face as a fresh wave of exhaustion swept through her body. Burying her face in her hands, Kelli sobbed, "I thought I was doing the right thing, honest I did."

Peter moved closer. "I'm sorry I yelled. It's not your fault—none of it," Peter argued. "I'm the one who dragged these children into the wilderness to live. I'm the one who agreed to your coming to this God-forsaken land in the first place. It's not your fault." Peter's distraught voice tugged at Kelli's sympathies.

She turned to face him. "You're right, you did. But, Peter, you didn't cause Pamela's appendix to inflame, and you had no control over the blizzard. Whether we'd been in Alaska or at my folks' home thirty miles from the nearest hospital, such an emergency could have occurred," Kelli argued, as she gesticulated her frustration through her waving hands. She searched his eyes, hoping her words were getting through. "Things happen—things none of us can predict. We can't take the credit or the blame."

"Peter," a voice outside the office door interrupted, "Suzanne says to come right away," Roger called.

He turned to leave. When Kelli started to follow, he suggested she rest. "I'll come and get you if you're needed," he said, then left the room.

The overstuffed sofa in one corner of Suzanne's office swallowed Kelli as she lay down. It felt so good to know that Pamela was in the hands of a competent physician, no longer her responsibility.

Even Lisa and Petey were being cared for by Roger. All she had to do was close her eyes and rest.

She was jarred awake as the office door flew open and Roger burst in. "Kelli, wake up. The plane's fueled, and Peter is ready to fly Pamela to Anchorage for emergency surgery. Suzanne wants your help since Pamela is asking for you. Lisa and Petey will stay with me."

Kelli sat up and rubbed her eyes. "Thanks, Roger, you're a great friend. But the storm. Can we fly in this storm?"

"I checked with the weather service. It's moving away from us," Roger said. "If Peter can get that crate off the ground, you'll be out of it in minutes."

Kelli grabbed her parka and ran to the airstrip. When she arrived, all were on board. Suzanne reached down and helped Kelli into the waiting plane, then climbed into the back seat with Pamela. "I'm glad you're going, Kelli. If she should take a turn for the worse, I'll need your help."

"Well, I hope I'm not needed, then," Kelli answered. "After all, I'm just along for the ride. Right, Kiddo?" She threw a big smile to Pamela, then snapped the seat belt closed across her lap.

"Sounds good to me." Suzanne wiped beads of sweat from the child's brow. "Hang in there, Pamela. We'll be at the hospital soon. You've been such a good girl. I'm so proud of you," Suzanne purred, soothing the frightened child's fears. "You are so brave."

Except for Suzanne's constant flow of encouragement, they rode in silence. When the lights of the city came into view, Kelli's exhausted mind finally relaxed. "We made it," she thought.

"Roger called ahead," Suzanne reminded, as the plane circled for a landing. "An ambulance will be waiting for us."

Even before the propellers stopped, the emergency team converged upon the plane and loaded Pamela and Suzanne into the emergency vehicle. As they roared off with sirens blaring, Kelli and Peter boarded the waiting patrol car.

Kelli's neck muscles had tightened like rivets on a gunboat. Her head throbbed from the tension. She turned her head from side to side.

"Lean on my shoulder," Peter suggested. "You look beat. It's in God's hands now, Kelli—and those paramedics in front of us," he reminded, as he pulled her against his shoulder.

Visions of the man she first met, the one who scoffed at her simple belief in answered prayer, flashed into her mind. Kelli smiled in spite of her fatigue. There'd been a change, she had to admit, and for the better. "Even if all I accomplish this year is to help Peter reestablish his faith in God, it will be worth it," she thought, though deep down inside she was hoping for more.

At the hospital, the medical team prepared Pamela for surgery while Peter signed the necessary admitting forms. An hour passed. Peter paced the small solarium. Kelli sat curled up on the vinyl sofa, pretending to read a fashion magazine.

Instead, she was praying, "Father, Pamela needs Your healing hand. Please guide Suzanne and the other doctors as they care for Your little one. And be with Peter. Keep his growing faith intact. Please help me to want these requests answered only if they are Your will. Amen."

When Suzanne entered the waiting room, her broad grin revealed the answer to their questions before she spoke.

"She's fine," Suzanne assured, taking them both into her arms. "I assisted Dr. Graves in surgery. The appendix probably would have burst within the hour. So, it was close. You saved her life, Kelli." She kissed Kelli's moist cheek. "You can wipe those tears away now. It's OK."

Kelli turned and walked to the window, overwhelmed with emotion. Behind her, Suzanne was talking with Peter. "The surgeon will talk with you in a few minutes," she explained. "Before you ask, Pamela's anesthetic hasn't worn off yet. You can see her in the morning. So, after the doctor leaves, you two go find a hotel and get some sleep," Suzanne scolded. "Oh, here he is now." She pointed to the doorway.

A tall graying man in operating room greens ambled in, looking tired, yet pleased. He answered all their questions then left.

When the surgeon disappeared from view, Suzanne shoved Peter and Kelli toward the door. "Now, you two, I'm staying in the doctor's lounge for the night. There's nothing either of you can do here at the hospital. A taxi is waiting out front. Go and get something to eat, then sleep! Doctor's orders."

Reluctantly they agreed. Peter helped Kelli into her parka, then guided her to the taxi. Her adrenalin supply had finally given out.

As she slid across the seat and rested her head on the opposite doorframe, Kelli felt like she'd been studying for college finals all night. She hardly noticed when Peter pulled her back against his shoulder. She thought she felt the moisture of a kiss on her forehead, but she was too far gone to know for certain.

Kelli slept during the ten-minute drive to the hotel. From somewhere beyond her, Kelli could hear Peter calling her, "Kelli, we're here. We're at the hotel, Kelli." He shook her gently. "I picked the closest one to the hospital I could find."

He paid the taxi driver then helped Kelli from the cab. Though the time seemed interminable to Kelli, she was settled in her second-floor room in a very short time. She tried to remember what time Peter had said he'd call for her in the morning and what room he said he was in should she need him. "Did he say 502?" she wondered. Almost immediately, she fell asleep fully dressed on the double bed.

A week of sunny days followed as Peter and Kelli traipsed back and forth to the hospital to be with Pamela. Because of the infection and the isolation of their home, Dr. Graves insisted on keeping the child in the hospital longer than was customary.

On Wednesday, as Kelli and Peter passed a small steepled church, she idly mentioned how much she missed attending regular church services since she'd come to Alaska. When Peter noticed the black-and-white sign on the lawn announcing a Wednesday evening prayer meeting, he insisted they attend.

The informal prayer service delighted Kelli more than she'd imagined possible. After the meeting, Peter talked for a few minutes with the pastor, while she wandered over to the piano and played one of her favorite hymns from the tattered hymnal.

"I do wish you two lived here in Anchorage," the short, balding pastor said as they prepared to leave. "We could use a young married couple like you in our congregation, especially you, Mrs. Karpenko, with your talents at the piano."

Kelli gulped and started to point out the minister's error when Peter encircled her waist with his arm. "Well, Pastor, we wish we could attend regularly too. But, well, as I told you earlier, my work makes it impossible."

They shook hands and parted. As Kelli and Peter walked down the icy steps to the sidewalk, she attacked. "How could you let that nice man think we are married?" she asked, her voice ascending the scale at a rapid rate.

Peter turned, shrugged his shoulders innocently, and said, "I didn't see any reason to correct him."

Kelli sighed dramatically. "I see every reason in the world!"

"Sorry," Peter mumbled, half apologetically, "I guess it might have been out of place."

The next morning Pamela was ready to go home. A festive reunion awaited her at the trading post. Not only did they celebrate Pamela's recovery, but the twins celebrated their eleventh birthday. The full-skirted, dotted swiss, spring dresses Kelli purchased on one of her shopping forays in Anchorage caused the girls to squeal with delight.

The girls had just blown out their candles when Roger handled Kelli a letter. "Here, this came for you this morning," he explained.

She looked at the fancy business head on the envelope and recognized it to be from Emerson Academy in Connecticut. Her heart sank as she read the unwelcome words.

*... and are counting on having you join our teaching staff in the fall as contracted. It might be wise for you to arrive on campus during the summer. This will give you time to organize your living quarters and acquaint yourself with the school and its policies before the fall term commences.
Sincerely,*

*Ms. Eliza M. McAuliffe
Headmistress, Emerson Academy
New Haven, Connecticut*

Kelli had always known this day would come—that reality would strike. But why now? she thought. Why today?

Chapter 14
Life in the Arctic

Kelli placed the girls' birthday gifts in a box in preparation for returning to the cabin.

"Kelli?" Suzanne called, stepping out of her office. "Roger agreed to take you back to the cabin, and he won't be ready for a few minutes. Can I talk with you for a bit?"

"Sure," Kelli answered, following Suzanne into her office. "What's up?"

The usually cool, sophisticated Suzanne blushed nervously then suggested, "You'd better sit down, I think." Kelli obeyed.

"I'm getting married," she announced, her face glowing with happiness. Kelli's mouth dropped open. She tried to speak, but no sound came out.

"Don't look so shocked. Jerry and I met at a medical convention last year, and we've been writing ever since. And this year at the convention in Seattle, well, we realized how much we cared for each other, and, well, he's willing to leave his practice in Michigan and move up here to be with me."

"But you never said a word about him," Kelli stuttered. "I mean, not one word."

"I know. I was afraid he was too good to be true. You know, after a woman goes through medical school and residency, the male population becomes sparse. And the men still available are either frightened off by a professional woman or are totally unappealing," she admitted with a grimace. "Jerry was engaged to be married when he was in college. But during a stint with the Peace Corps, the gal jilted him. It's taken him a long time to trust another woman—lucky for me, I might add."

Kelli shook her head in wonder. "I'm very happy for you. When's the wedding?"

"Oh, probably in July sometime. We haven't set a date yet," Suzanne explained. "I'd like you to be my maid of honor."

Kelli smiled sadly. "Oh, Suzanne, I'd love to, but I'll probably be back East by then, at my new teaching appointment."

"No," Suzanne groaned. "I'd so hoped you could. The wedding will be held in Seattle at my parents' home church. I understand though."

"You know I would if I could," Kelli began.

"Somehow I got the impression that you and Peter," she paused, "well, you know. You seemed like a good match to me."

Kelli shook her head sadly. "No, his wife, Liz, is still very much alive in his mind, I'm afraid. He's made that quite clear."

"That's too bad," Suzanne sympathized. "I do know that something's bugging him badly. Lately, when we're out on our medical runs, he wanders off by himself for hours without any explanation. That's not the wisest behavior in these parts."

Kelli bit her lip and shrugged her shoulders helplessly. "I—I—I'm sorry," she whispered.

"Forgive me for asking, but how do you feel about him?" Suzanne queried.

Kelli hesitated, then mumbled, "I'm not sure." Her eyes pleaded for Suzanne to understand.

"You know what, I think you are surer than you care to admit," Suzanne said. "Take it from the voice of experience."

Kelli paled, her eyes shouting what her lips refused to say.

The sound of Roger's voice was a welcome relief for Kelli.

"For a time, I'd hoped you and my brother would get something going," Suzanne admitted.

Kelli smiled. "Just friends," she explained.

"I understand. Same with Peter and me. He's been a lifesaver this year, chaperoning me around this part of Alaska," Suzanne mused.

The two women jumped at the sound of a heavy knock on the door. "Hey, you two women done gossiping yet?" Roger bellowed, "I'm all ready to take you gals home anytime."

"Be right there," Kelli replied, turning toward Suzanne. "Please, don't mention how I feel about Peter to anyone, OK?"

"Are you sure?" Suzanne asked.

"I'm sure," Kelli responded.

On the flight back to the Karpenko cabin, the children kept the conversation lively, leaving Kelli to mull over her latest discovery about herself.

The next few days moved by slowly for everyone. The daily temperatures were too low to allow the children to play outside. Cabin fever had set in.

One morning after the studies were completed, Lisa suggested, "Miss Kelli, let's have a teaparty or something."

Pamela's eyes lighted up immediately. "We could all dress up, maybe even put on a play."

"Wait a minute," Kelli began.

"Yeah, we could write our own script, for one of our English assignments," Lisa suggested.

"That's dumb!" Petey continued building his block city. Everything was "dumb" to Petey lately.

"Oh hush, Petey. I just got a great idea," Pamela added. "But I want to surprise you. Could we do it? Could we?"

"Could we, huh? Please? Pretty please?" Lisa begged, their ponytails bouncing in perfect syncopation.

They have completed all their formal school work. They're weeks ahead of schedule, Kelli reasoned. Why not? she thought. Maybe it will get me out of the doldrums too. She scowled, pretending for a moment to think ill of the idea. Then her face brightened. "I think it's a good idea. What would you like to do?"

"Leave it all to us. We will plan everything, right down to the tea cakes," Pamela airily assured her.

Closeted committee meetings and secret caucuses sprang up all over the house for days. When the twins instructed Roger to bring a long shopping list of special food supplies, he joined in on their conspiracy.

Kelli enjoyed watching the two girls carry out their plans. Before long, Petey warmed up to the adventure too.

When Lisa delivered a hand-printed invitation to Kelli, she also delivered with it definite instructions on Kelli's apparel. "You must wear your red dress. You know, the one I like so much."

On the big day, Kelli awoke to the smell of cookies baking. Beside the bed, she found a small bell with a note attached, instructing her to ring for service. She dutifully complied.

Almost instantly, her bedroom door flew open and Pamela entered, carrying a tray. On the tray was a small vase of dried flowers with a breakfast of scrambled eggs, toast, and orange juice. When Kelli finished her meal, Lisa informed her that a bubble bath was ready. After Kelli dressed, Petey arrived with an armload of books from the trading post's lending library.

"Obviously I am restricted to my quarters," she noted.

"That's right," he announced importantly.

Lunch arrived at the stroke of twelve. Petey stayed to keep her company while she ate.

"When am I to be let out of isolation?" Kelli questioned.

The little boy shrugged his shoulders, dumped his building blocks onto the floor, and began constructing a skyscraper. The afternoon was as uneventful as the morning.

After Pamela brought her a light snack, Kelli was advised to dress for an evening at the "Karpenko Dinner Theater." Secretly, she was glad for an excuse to wear her red dress. It had been a long time since she had been able to dress up.

Artfully, she sculptured her shoulder-length brown curls high onto her head, pinning each one into place. After spraying perfume in her hair and on her wrists and neck, she slipped into her matching pumps and prepared for her grand entrance. The audience of three oohed and ahhhed with delight as she descended the stairs.

"You're beautiful, Miss Kelli," Petey whispered. "I'm going to marry you when I grow up."

"If Uncle Roger doesn't marry her first," Lisa suggested.

"You two haven't any idea of what you're talking about," Pamela sniffed. "He's going to marry me!" With that Pamela exited the room.

The candlelight meal, though somewhat unbalanced nutritionally, was delicious. Kelli complimented the children repeatedly. When it came time to clean up, they refused her help.

"If you really want to help, you can put away the dishes while we get into our costumes," Pamela suggested.

When she agreed, the children raced through the house, turning off lights and adjusting their makeshift stage curtains for added secrecy. In the kitchen, Kelli gazed at the dancing flames on the long white tapers, reluctant to blow them out and ruin the atmosphere. "I'll leave them for just a few minutes longer," she thought, as she tied a dish towel about her waist, "at least until I wash off all the counters and the table top."

As she reached across the table, a curl slipped from its pin. Ignoring it, she picked up one candlestick and washed beneath it. Suddenly she sensed she was being watched. She looked up to find Peter leaning against the doorjamb.

"How long have you been there?" Kelli asked. "Why are you here? When did you get home? Are you hungry?"

"One question at a time. I'll try to answer you, in reverse. No, I'm not hungry; I ate at the Lee's. I just got home, five minutes ago. I'm here because Roger insisted you needed me. And I've been standing here—long enough," he added. "Now it's my turn. Why did Roger say you needed me? Who told you that I love red dresses? Mmm, what brand of perfume are you wearing? I like it."

"Long enough for what?" she demanded, regarding him suspiciously.

"I answered your questions. Now it's your turn. You don't get to ask extra questions," he drawled, coming around the corner of the table. "First about Roger—"

"I have no idea why Roger made up such a story. And as for this," she looked down at her dress, iridescent in the candlelight, "your children are planning a night at the theater and insisted I dress up," she explained, self-consciously yanking the dish towel from her waist. "Oh yes, and I'm wearing Windswept." She was hopeful that the candlelight concealed the inordinate amount of color rising in her cheeks. "We'd better go into the living room. We wouldn't want to miss any of the show," she said, leaning over to blow out the candles. As she extinguished one candle, he blew out the other, leaving them face to face in the moonlight. Her dark eyes, filled with unanswered questions, widened as she stared across the table at Peter's equally unreadable expression. For a moment, all motion ceased.

Suddenly Peter stood up and flipped on the light switch. Kelli blinked at the suddenly blinding florescent light.

"Oh, Kelli." Peter ran his fingers through his hair in frustration. "What am I going to do? I've never met anyone who can scramble my brain so badly. What I want to do and what I have to do are so far apart. I should be pushing you into my best friend's arms."

"I resent that," she began. "I'm not a toy to pass between friends. I'm a woman, capable of—" the sound of approaching feet ended the conversation.

"We're ready," Pamela peeked her head around the corner of the doorway. Her eyes widened in surprise as she squealed, "Oh, goody! Daddy made it in time for the play."

"So you're the one who told Uncle Roger to send me home." Peter nodded knowingly. "I'm glad you did. It looks like someone has gone to a lot of trouble to make this a special night."

"We didn't want you to miss the opening performance," Pamela replied.

"OK, you just said it's curtain time. The show must go on," he joked, allowing Pamela to lead him to the couch where Lisa was already seating Kelli.

From the time the curtains opened until the end of the performance, the two-member audience couldn't stop laughing, though Kelli spent part of the time shrinking in embarrassment.

The play, entitled *Life in the Arctic*, graphically depicted humorous and not so humorous incidents that had happened since Kelli arrived. When his cue came, Benjamin refused to cooperate by jumping into the hood of Kelli's bathrobe worn by Pamela, no matter how much Petey coaxed. Wrapped in a brown wool blanket, Lisa played the attacking bear to perfection.

Kelli noticed that Peter didn't seem too pleased when Petey played the flirting Roger Lee delivering Wednesday's groceries. She was thankful, however, that Pamela acted true to Kelli's character when rebuffing him.

As the children began the final scene of the play, two of the actors suddenly dissolved into tears and rushed for the audience.

"Oh, Miss Kelli, you can't leave us," Lisa begged, throwing herself into Kelli's arms. "We need you so much."

"Don't go, Miss Kelli. Don't go." Petey buried his face in her shoulder.

Pamela stood by the piano, somewhat stunned by the sudden turn of events. Kelli realized that Pamela hadn't planned the evening to end quite this way. A strange indecision surfaced in the child's eyes.

Peter interrupted, "Children, you're not being fair to Miss Kelli. She has plans. There are people in her life that are important to her. She's made commitments that we have no right to ask her to break," he said, stroking his daughter's tear-stained cheek. "She's shared a good part of a year of her life with us. That's quite a lot really. And she's brought us so much love and happiness. What more can we ask?"

"That she stay!" Petey pouted.

Kelli lifted the little boy's face toward hers. "Hey, what's going on? Why the tears? This is a party, remember? Besides we still have a couple more months to be together, right?" Kelli tickled Lisa under her chin. "And thank you for tonight. I've enjoyed every minute of it."

"Miss Kelli," Pamela shifted nervously from one foot to the other, "will you play the piano and sing for us out of Grandma's old love-song books? You sing too, Daddy."

Though the children attempted to sing the old tunes, one by one, they stopped to listen as Kelli's rich alto voice harmonized with Peter's smooth baritone on the unfamiliar tunes.

"Don't throw bouquets at me . . . people will say we're in love." Kelli and Peter were enjoying themselves so much they failed to notice that they had acquired an audience instead of a backup chorus.

"Do you know this one?" Peter turned the page and pointed to one of his old-time favorites. She nodded and began the introduction.

Kelli played while Peter sang, "When other nights, and other days will find us gone our separate ways, we'll have these moments. . . ." He stopped. Kelli glanced up from the music. His face was pale, yet he managed to finish the song in a whisper, " . . . to remember."

"Bad choice," he mumbled. Then in a commanding voice he announced, "OK, Kids, it's getting late. Up to bed." Bewildered at the sudden mood shift, Pamela and Lisa hurried to obey. Petey started to protest, but recognized the stubborn expression on his father's face and ran to catch up with his sisters.

"I'm sorry! It's been a long day. I'm bushed. Excuse me please. I've got to get back down to Lee's place in order to get a good night's sleep." He crossed the room and closed the library door behind him.

The notes on the page gyrated crazily before Kelli's eyes as she tried to piece the events of the evening into some sort of perspective. Nothing made sense, especially Peter's strange behavior. Distraught, Kelli buried her head in her arms and prayed, "I'm so confused, Lord. I don't know what's happening between Peter and me, if anything. I don't want to think of leaving—of never seeing him or the children again! Help me, Lord—*please?*" The tears she had wiped from Petey's eyes earlier, now trickled from her own.

Chapter 15
Letting Go

Pamela scowled. "I don't understand it. It doesn't make sense," she wailed, her lower lip protruding angrily.

"Come on, it's not that difficult. First, though, you're going to have to get rid of the idea that you can't understand math. Your hardest battle is not percentages, but attitude," Kelli reminded. "Let's try again."

"Kelli," Peter called from the foot of the stairs, "could you come to the library, please?"

"Fine," she answered, "I'll be right down. Let's put the math away for now and do your reading assignment while I'm talking with your dad. And, Lisa, when you finish your geography assignment, work on your essay, OK?"

The morning had started out with everyone helping to clean up from the party of the night before, everyone except Peter. He returned from the Lee's around nine o'clock. And by the sound of his voice, he didn't appear any too cheerful. Kelli hurried to the library, where she found him standing behind his desk.

"Close the door, please," he said, waving her toward the chair in front of the desk.

"First, I have some good news. I got word this morning that my mother's surgery went well," he announced. "They found a small tumor at the base of her skull, and, thank God, it was benign. She'll be staying with friends while she recuperates."

A look of shock crossed Kelli's face. "Surgery? You didn't say she was scheduled for surgery," Kelli exclaimed.

"I didn't want to upset the children prematurely," he explained. "I've made arrangements with my aunt in Seattle. She has agreed to care for the children until I complete my research in June."

Kelli straightened in her chair, uncertain of what he was saying. "What? What are you trying to tell me?" she demanded.

"I've done a lot of thinking, and I've decided that leaving you alone with the children for such long periods of time is unwise. I've appreciated you very much. You're the best thing that's happened to this family in a long time," he admitted, while staring at the blotter on his desktop.

He eyed Kelli as she walked over to the window. "Although I've enjoyed having my family close at hand these past few months, I can't be so irresponsible as to jeopardize your life or that of my children any longer."

"When did you decide all this?" she asked.

"As I said, I've been thinking about it for some time now," he repeated.

"OK. How soon do I leave, Dr. Karpenko?" she snapped.

"Kelli," his voice strained with tension, "I thought we were friends."

"So did I," she mused aloud. "Why do I have the feeling that you're not leveling with me?"

He thought for a full minute before answering, "You're right, I'm not being entirely truthful, mainly because I'm confused myself. Perhaps it's time we really talk." He got up from the desk and walked to her side. "Sit down," he said, pointing to the leather recliner.

Kelli bristled at the authoritarian tone in his voice. She pursed her lips, glancing coldly toward him, which made him amend his request. "I'm sorry. Please sit down, Kelli."

Reluctantly, she complied.

"Kelli," he began, throwing his head back and taking a deep breath, "this is going to be tougher than I imagined."

She waited for him to continue.

"Do you remember the first night you arrived, after you hit me with the book?" A tiny smile quivered at the corners of his mouth.

Though she tried not to, Kelli smiled and looked away.

"I told you I never wanted to marry again," he reminded, dropping to the footstool in front of her.

Kelli studied the condition of her fingernails.

"I still feel that way," he admitted. "For a time, Liz's death stripped me of all caring, even for the children. I didn't ever want to love another human being again." Peter ran his hands through his hair, then continued. "My mother is the reason the children came to Alaska with me. I just wanted to walk out and disappear into the north woods. She wouldn't let me. Then she insisted you come," he paused, resting his forehead in his hands. "I resisted, but not enough. When you arrived with your copper-brown eyes and smile that could melt the polar ice cap, I was afraid. I knew

I should send you packing right from the first, but instead I sat back and watched as one by one, you dazzled each member of my family, including Pamela."

Peter paused to clear his throat. "Before you came, I carried Liz with me everywhere I went. I could see her running along a California beach, dodging waves. I pictured her diving off the high dive at the university pool, swimming over to me and—But lately, those memories are fading. Slowly but surely, I'm losing Liz. You can't possibly understand, but I'm scared to let go."

"Peter," Kelli interrupted, "please, I don't need to know—"

"Yes you do!" he snapped. "Don't you see? Half of me is falling in love with you, and the other half is saying, 'Don't be stupid!' "

"And what am I supposed to say?" Kelli asked. "For what it's worth, I care about you, too, and I hate to see you stuck in a time warp." She gazed intently into his eyes, then shook her head sadly, "I love you, Peter, but I would never give my heart to a man who cannot return that love. Liz must have been a wonderful woman, but I refuse to live in her shadow. So you're quite safe."

Kelli stood up and crossed the room. "Someday, Peter, you've got to let go of the past and let God heal your heart. I'll be praying for you."

Opening the door, she added, "And I hope whoever the woman is who prompts that decision—I hope she realizes the value of what she's getting." Her chin quivered, but she stood firm. "And now, would you book my flight to Portland as soon as possible?" she asked, closing the door as she left.

On the morning of Kelli's departure, she stacked her luggage by the front door, then angled into the library. After touching her favorite books on the shelves, she ran her hand across the back of the leather chair for a moment.

In the living room, she straightened the throw pillows one more time, then climbed the stairs to her room.

Once there, Kelli removed a tissue from her pocket and blew her nose. Her thoughts suddenly turned to her white porcelain framed motto. "If you love something, let it go. . . ." Abruptly she walked to the window and fluffed the curtains, then removed an imaginary wrinkle from the quilt on her bed. Idly she set the rocking chair rocking—temporarily lost in her memories. She failed to hear Peter ascend the stairs.

"We've got to go, Kelli," he reminded softly, "to make your connecting flight, that is."

She bit her lip and dotted her eyes with the tissue. "Are the children—"

"They're already on board," he explained. "Maybe this wasn't such a—"

"Right." She made one last sweep of the room, memorizing every detail. "Let's go," she announced, brushing past him into the hall. He put out his hand for a moment, then withdrew before touching her arm. She ignored the gesture and walked stoically down the stairs.

Once in the plane, she avoided looking at the three pairs of reddened eyes and downcast faces in the back seat.

"Well, I'll bet you children are anxious to see your Auntie Helen again," Kelli sputtered at machine-gun speed. "Seattle's a fun place to visit. I'll bet one of the first things she'll do is to take you to the Space Needle. Won't that be fun?" Her only answer was the sound of random sniffles.

The plane took off and circled back around the landing strip, heading toward Anchorage. She strained to catch a last view of the cabin in the clearing, the lake, the storage shed at the end of the landing strip. Barely moving her fingers, Kelli waved goodbye, knowing the memory would have to last a lifetime. "Maybe letting go will more difficult to do than to talk about," she thought, glancing toward Peter's stone-cold profile. "Not just for him, but for me too."

Chapter 16
Time to Retreat

Kelli glanced up at the framed motto on the night table by her bed and sighed. "If you love something, set it free...." She thought about the times she'd glibly uttered those words, never imagining the courage it took to live them. Removing her Bible from her nightstand, she opened it to her favorite promise, "In all thy ways ..." Since returning home, she'd begun all her personal devotions with the same prayer request: faith to trust—to believe that God was indeed guiding her life.

She recited the text again, forcing herself to remember all the times when God had obviously led in her life. And with each memory she thanked Him again. Yet Peter and the children continued to invade her dreams at night and her thoughts during the day.

Her parents worried yet remained silent, knowing that when the time was right, she'd talk.

Each morning, at the sound of the mail truck, Kelli raced to the mailbox, hoping for a letter or a card postmarked Alaska. None came. After eight weeks, she stopped, deciding the time had come to get on with her life.

"Mom, I think I'll take the headmistress' suggestion and arrive early on campus. I'd like to be settled before school begins," Kelli explained. "Daddy promised to help me find a good second-hand car. Then I'll take my time driving across the States." Kelli took a deep sigh, then continued, "Dr. Karpenko's check will easily cover my travel expenses, plus establish a healthy bank account for emergencies."

"I'm just getting used to having you home again," her mother interrupted, her eyes filling with sadness.

"I know, but I guess I'm not happy wherever I am right now," Kelli explained.

"I don't know what happened in Alaska. I wish you could confide in Daddy or me. We've both been praying for you, though," Mother admitted, searching Kelli's face for clues to the girl's thinking. "Just don't run ahead of God, Sweetheart."

Kelli hugged her mother warmly and whispered, "Thanks for understanding and being so patient with me. Before I leave, I'll tell you everything—at least what there is to tell."

Mr. Saunders threw himself enthusiastically into the task of car shopping. The final choice, a fire-red Toyota, pleased them both. And for the next few evenings, Kelli became the son her father had always wanted. He lectured her on the care and feeding of her "little red monster"—as she called it.

One evening, as Kelli scrubbed motor oil from her hands, she told him, "I think I should take the monster on a short run before making the long trip east—maybe to the coast or down to the redwoods. What do you think?"

He stroked his chin for a moment. "Sounds good to me. Do you want me to go with you?" he asked.

"That would defeat my purpose. I need to see if I can manage alone."

"S'pose you're right," he demurred.

Suddenly the telephone rang. "Peter!" she thought. Hope swirled through her. She dropped everything and ran for the phone.

"Hello?" she answered, holding her breath in anticipation.

"Hello, Kelli, is your father home?" the church pastor asked.

"Oh, yes, Pastor Michaels," Kelli replied, trying to hide the disappointment in her voice. "Hold on, please, I'll get him."

She handed the receiver to her father and stumbled into the living room. Upon seeing her mother, Kelli rushed into the woman's arms.

"I'm hurting so badly," she cried. "I've done everything I can to give God free reign in my life and in Peter's. Intellectually, I accept things as they are, but emotionally, I just can't. . . . Oh, Mama, I never want to love again!"

Her mother held the girl in her arms and massaged the tight, knotted muscles in Kelli's neck and shoulders. "Give yourself time," the woman advised.

"My problem is that I don't want to heal," Kelli admitted. "I want Peter!"

Lifting Kelli's chin with her fingertips, her mother looked into her eyes. "Even if Peter is not God's man for you?" Mother asked.

"Why does it have to be this way?" Kelli begged for an easy answer.

"I don't know, Honey. I honestly don't know."

Kelli held nothing back, sharing the entire story with her parents. Finally she confessed, "That's why I want to be alone for a few days. I've got to take my own advice and let go within my mind. I thought walking among those big trees would put things into perspective. I'm beginning to understand the pain Peter has suffered losing Liz, and why he's reluctant to risk loving again."

After talking and praying together, sheer exhaustion forced them to retire. Unburdening herself to her parents had indeed helped. Somehow knowing others knew and cared made her pain easier to bear.

The next morning, Kelli spread the California/Oregon map out on the hood of her car and carefully reviewed her travel itinerary with her parents. "I thought I'd detour up the coast by Gold Beach and Bandon, get a motel room somewhere along here tonight. Then head down to Redwood National Park, spend the day, find lodging for the night, and return home late the following day."

Mrs. Saunders loaded a huge wicker basket of food onto the passenger's seat. Kelli kissed her parents goodbye and headed down the driveway, waving to her parents until they were out of sight. The time for tears was over. It was time to retreat.

Chapter 17
When Love Returns

Kelli stopped at every overlook and walked along every beach she came to. She had to admit that having only herself to care for was a new experience—almost fun, at least for a couple of days. After settling her things into her motel room, she had a light supper from the lunch her mother had packed and headed down to the beach to enjoy the sunset. It was dark, and Kelli was exhausted by the time she returned to the empty motel room.

The next morning, she awakened to the pounding surf and the squawking sea gulls outside her window. She stretched, grabbed her robe, and headed into the shower.

"OK, the pity party is over, Miss Saunders," she announced, throwing open her suitcase and removing her favorite lavender sundress. "Today, no jeans! Today, you will be glamorous!" she announced, then laughed, "Within reason, of course."

With a spring in her step and summer in the air, she emerged from the motel room into the morning sunshine.

"Ah, gorgeous," she sighed, twirling about once and skipping down the stairs. After dumping her case and mom's half-empty basket into the trunk, she drove to a small café for breakfast.

When she reached the corridor of redwoods, they were as breathtaking as she'd remembered. She followed the highway until she came to her favorite spot in the entire park. There she parked the car and got out to walk around. She was alone. She could hardly believe her good fortune. Her very own cathedral! Scowling at her spaghetti-strap sandals, Kelli decided against glamour in favor of her sand-infested sneakers.

A gentle breeze rustled her hair and caressed her cheek. "Ah, this is heaven," she thought.

The sound of children's voices in the distance alerted Kelli that her sanctuary had been invaded. "Oh well," she sighed, stepping up her pace, "it had to happen sooner or later."

Kelli's attention was drawn to a flash of red ahead on the trail. Her heart stopped at the sound of a familiar voice, "Miss Kelli! Miss Kelli!"

Speechless, she stopped in the middle of the path as Petey hurled himself down the path and into her arms. When chubby arms circled her neck, she realized that it wasn't a dream.

"Petey! What are you doing here?" she screeched, tears glistening in her eyes.

He wriggled from her grasp. "We came to getcha," he squealed, then ran back down the pathway. "Here she is! I found her! Over here, Lisa, see? I knew I could find her," he shouted. Screams of delight filled the forest as Lisa and Pamela raced to her side.

She tried to embrace all three children at once. "It is you. Lisa, Petey, Pamela! I can't believe it. What are you doing here? How did you find me?"

Pamela giggled, "Your mamma sent us," she said. "We stayed all night at your house. Lisa and I slept in your bedroom. I got your bed. Lisa slept in Rhonda's," Pamela explained.

"My parents? You were in Medford? Why?" Kelli struggled to make some sense of what they were trying to tell her.

"How else could we find you?" Lisa asked matter-of-factly.

Kelli caressed each of their faces tenderly. "I missed you all so much. Pamela," she cooed, "Lisa, and Petey."

"Miss Kelli, you left before my birthday," Petey accused. "I'm six years old. And I'm too old to be called Petey now. My name is Pete or Peter, like my father," he explained. Kelli paused as she became aware, wildly hoping—

"If we're going to change names," Pamela added, "could you call me Pam?"

"I'd love to, Pam. And Petey, you shall be Pete from now on," Kelli agreed soberly. "Did my mother bring you to find me?" Kelli hardly dare breathe as she awaited their answer.

"Oh, no, she gave Daddy directions for where to find you," Pete announced.

"Oh! We forgot about Daddy," Lisa gasped. "I'll go get him," she volunteered.

Pam grabbed Lisa and pointed. "Never mind; he's coming," Pam said.

Kelli paled. Her heart surfaced to her throat as she watched the tall, lithe man in trim gray pants and black polo shirt saunter toward them.

When he first noticed Kelli and the children standing beside one of the trees, he paused then proceeded slowly toward them.

Once he was within easy hearing range, he called, "Well, they did find you, didn't they?" A nervous grin played across his face.

Kelli opened her mouth to reply, but the words stuck in her throat. "I—I—I—It's so nice to see you again, Dr. Karpenko," she stuttered.

"We missed you," he said, ignoring her formal greeting. Then, taking one of her hands in his, he continued. "More specifically, I missed you. It took Suzanne and Roger to talk turkey to me, followed by two weeks in the back country alone with God, before I realized just how much I really missed you." He examined her manicured fingernails for a moment. "I want to thank you for bringing God back into my life, Kelli."

"Dad," Pete interrupted, pulling on his father's trouser leg.

"Son," Peter began, "Miss Kelli and I have some things to talk over. Will you please go to the car with your sisters and wait there?"

The little boy nodded, turned, and followed his two sisters without question.

Taking advantage of the interruption, Kelli slipped her hand out of Peter's and walked to the far side of the tree. "I don't understand," she said.

"It was after I left the children with my aunt in Seattle and put the cabin up for sale." He came up behind her speaking as he approached. "Suzanne helped me see the happiness that could be mine if I let go of Liz's memory. And Roger threatened to find you himself if I didn't," he added, noting the slight blush on Kelli's cheeks. "Well, I got angry and stormed out—determined to go alone. I was at the furthest point on my circuit, at least a mile and a half from the plane when I accidently twisted my ankle by falling off an embankment." Peter grasped Kelli's upper arm as he continued. "It was pretty bad—thought it was broken. There was no one around to help, and it was close to dusk. At that moment, I felt no one would even care if I didn't return. I had a lot of time to think as I lay there beside the trail, enough to realize that for the first time since Liz's death, I didn't want to die," he said. "I wanted to live. I really wanted to live."

"Oh, Peter," Kelli whispered, her eyes shining with joy. "I'm so glad. I've been praying so hard for you."

Peter squeezed Kelli's arm and smiled. "First, I prayed for God to help me; then I remembered Liz. Suddenly, all the anger I'd stored inside came out. I shouted at God. I don't know how long I was lying there before I realized I had nowhere to turn, but I claimed your favorite promise. 'In all thy ways acknowledge him, and he shall direct thy paths.' And then, one at a time, I began to say Thank You for the children, for my mother, for Suzanne and Roger's friendship, and most of all, for you."

Kelli's clasped her hands tightly together.

"When I finished, I felt a wave of peace fill me. And instead of worrying about my precarious situation, I actually fell asleep." He paused, his voice husky with emotion. "Some time later I awoke to the sound of whistling. I shouted for help, and an old prospector found me. He wrapped my swollen ankle in an old shirt and helped me walk the mile and a half to the plane." Peter added, "I know God sent that old sourdough to save my life."

Tears glistened in Kelli's eyes; her throat constricted.

"When I got back to the trading post, I spent the next three days tabulating my latest research, then returned to the lower forty-eight," Peter explained.

Almost without breathing, Kelli waited for him to continue. Gently, he placed his hands on her shoulders and turned her around to face him. "Kelli, I believe God led you to Alaska. It wasn't chance that sent you to the college office that afternoon my mother's letter arrived. And it was also no accident that I grew to love you." His eyes bored into hers with such intensity that she felt it necessary to look away. "You hadn't been gone more than a week when I realized what a fool I'd been to discourage that love. I was scared," he admitted, lifting his gaze beyond her face, "scared to love again."

"I didn't want to write or call. I had to explain everything to your face." He shrugged. "So the children and I hopped a jet to Medford. We arrived at your folks' place yesterday afternoon. You have great parents, Kelli."

Kelli smiled and nodded. "Thanks, they've helped me a lot since—" she stopped, quickly changing the subject. "By the way, how did Daddy act toward you?" she asked, her eyes dark with concern.

"At first, your father was rather distant," Peter admitted, grinning knowingly, "but when I explained to him how much I love you, he warmed up considerably."

"I—I—you—you—" Kelli stammered at his last statement and cleared her throat.

"Have you always had such a speech impediment? I never noticed it before," he teased. "Anyway, as I was saying, your folks and I stayed up last night talking. I wanted to look for you then, but your mother suggested I wait until today since searching through Redwood National Forest might prove simpler than cruising the entire southern Oregon coast." Again he smiled, tilting her face toward his. "Kelli, I do love you. And I am no longer trying to live with a ghost. I need you, a real live woman, by my side today and for as many tomorrows as we'll be allowed. I just hope it isn't too late."

"But, Peter, I have responsibilities—a teaching contract in Connecticut," Kelli reminded, her face clouding with anguish.

"Sweetheart, I have two years in which to write up the results of my research. Connecticut is as good a place as any in which to do it."

Kelli searched his eyes, scarcely believing what she heard.

He continued, "And if two years isn't enough time—"

"Two years," she breathed.

"I don't want to take your love for granted or demand more than you're ready to commit," Peter explained, his face serious with concern. "For my part, I've not a doubt in the world," he said, pausing to search her face for the answers to his unspoken questions, "but we both want God to lead in our relationship. And you are a lot younger than I, so perhaps you will need—"

"Peter," Kelli growled threateningly, as she turned to grasp his throat between her hands.

He raised his arms to protect himself and laughed. "Just kidding, just kidding," he protested.

"Humph!" she muttered, "Knowing you, you'll still be lamenting my 'tender' age when I'm rocking our grandchildren to sleep on my lap!"

"Grandchildren already?" he taunted, smiling down at her as she strolled by his side. "Sounds like you're willing to risk a few more years than just two."

"Humph!" Kelli arched one eyebrow skeptically. "I don't know. A man of your advancing years can hardly plan too far into the future, can he?" she teased, batting her eyelashes innocently.

After clearing his throat, Peter grinned and placed his arm around her shoulders. Then, in a high-pitched, shaky voice, he replied, "Granny, will you help your old hubby-to-be hobble back to the wagon before he gets much older?"

Kelli giggled as she slipped her arm about Peter's waist. "We can make it, old man," she teased.

Peter drew her closer to his side and whispered, "Honey, together we can make it—anywhere." And arm in arm, they ambled down the trail to the waiting children and toward the unspoken promises of tomorrow.